A CONCISE GUIDE IN COLOUR

Decorative House Plants

by Jaroslav Oplt

Illustrated by
Jiřina Kaplická

HAMLYN

LONDON · NEW YORK · SYDNEY · TORONTO

Translated by Olga Kuthanová
Designed and produced by Artia for
THE HAMLYN PUBLISHING GROUP LIMITED
London - New York - Sydney - Toronto
Astronaut House, Feltham, Middlesex, England
Copyright © Artia 1976
Second impression 1977
ISBN 0 600 34481 9.
Printed in Czechoslovakia
3/02/29/51-02

CONTENTS

FOREWORD

In this book the reader will find instructions for the cultivation and propagation of 88 ornamental house plants. Flowers, the same as books and music, are a continual source of pleasure and that is why they are grown by so many people, especially those living in large cities.

The selection given here includes not only plants that are easy to grow and thus popular with beginners but also ones with more demanding requirements for the experienced grower. Some of the described species are very tender and their cultivation indoors may appear to be practically impossible, but with a good knowledge of their needs the grower can achieve very satisfactory results.

In many private homes one sees magnificent specimens of which even a professional grower could be proud. They are plants rarely seen even in shops. Bearing in mind the inventiveness of amateur growers, who are attracted by the rare exotic plant, this book endeavours to bring the cultivation and propagation of these plants within their reach as well. Modern interior design demands new types of house plants, ones which, as yet, are considered exotic but will soon be viewed as common ornamentals. This book wishes to share with readers valuable information about growing plants in homes with central heating, in air-conditioned public buildings and hotels as well as in places of work.

Many people lose heart with their first failure and do not try to find out why their plants died. To meet with as few disappointments as possible one must remember that every plant has different requirements, chiefly with regard to soil, light, warmth and moisture.

The aim of this book is to provide every would-be

grower of house plants with at least the basic know-how of cultivation, to advise what kinds are suitable for various conditions, and how to arrange and care for them so that they are a source of pleasure the whole year round.

BASIC REQUIREMENTS OF HOUSE PLANT CULTIVATION

House plants may be said to be domesticated plants, since they will not grow without our care and attention. Before setting out to acquire some, therefore, it is necessary to learn something about the conditions under which they grow in their native habitat. Most important are their light, moisture and heat requirements, the medium in which they should be grown, how they can be propagated, how they should be protected against pests, and where they should be placed.

LIGHT

One often notices how different are the leaves, shape and height of plants of the same species grown in different locations. Though their growth is influenced by all the basic factors simultaneously the difference in their appearance is mainly due to the amount of light available.

Reliable information about light requirements may be acquired only from a knowledge of the plant's natural habitat or from its appearance. In general, it may be said that hard leathery leaves, felted leaves, grey-green leaves with a wax coat, etc., are characteristics of plants that tolerate lots of sun. On the other hand, plants with delicate or pale green foliage require shade and often are intolerant of direct sunlight. Only very few plants will thrive in the corners of dark rooms and in such cases artificial light is beneficial. There are many plants that can be grown successfully in rooms with north-facing windows, including ferns, clivias, primulas and palms. Most house plants thrive if placed by a window which gets either the morning or afternoon sun.

It is also important to know the period of daylight each individual plant requires in order to flower. In this respect plants are divided into three separate groups: those that require short periods of daylight to flower, those that require long periods of daylight to flower, and those whose flowering is not dependent on the day's length. Plants of the first group can be made to flower sooner and out of their natural season by darkening the room and thus shortening the day's length. In plants of the second group, which normally flower in summer, flowering can be regulated by providing additional light, e. g. pelargoniums can be made to bloom even in winter if their 'day' is prolonged by artificial light to as much as twelve hours, which is the day's length throughout the year in their native habitat.

WATER

Water is another of the basic factors affecting a plant's growth. Soil moisture requirements are determined by the plant's native habitat. Some tropical plants require moisture all the year round, others are adapted to cope with regular periods of drought, and still others, e. g. certain cacti, grow in a dry environment throughout the year. Correct watering is the real measure of a grower's knowledge. Watering should be governed by the individual needs of the plants under cultivation and, therefore, the water requirements change in relation to the age of the plant, the time of the day and the season of the year, as well as the weather, light and temperature. In general, plants in full growth require more water than those in the juvenile stage.

When the temperature decreases so does the plant's ability to absorb water and a too-plentiful supply at lower temperatures is damaging to the roots and, therefore, to the whole plant. On the other hand, when the temperature rises evaporation increases and the plant requires more water. During the warm summer months, especially on hot days, water should be supplied more frequently. During cold periods, when plants need less moisture, they should be given only enough water to meet their immediate requirements. If potted plants are plunged in soil, peat, moss or similar material in an ornamental container they will require less water than free-standing specimens.

Plants that are grown in light soil which does not retain moisture, e. g. azaleas, camellias and ferns, may easily dry up. For plants growing in clay pots it is possible to determine whether the soil is dry or not by knocking on the pot with the knuckles; if the sound has a ringing tone then water is required. Another guideline is the pot's weight — if it is light then that means that the soil is dry and the plant should be given water. This applies to both clay and plastic pots. The best method of watering an over-dry plant is to immerse the pot in a bucket of water and leave it until water can be seen to have soaked through the compost in the pot.

Plants that dry out easily, particularly in small pots, can be kept in a moist atmosphere by standing them in a larger, ornamental container and filling the space between the pot and container with moss, which should be kept moist according to need. It often happens that a plant wilts even though it is watered thoroughly. In such a case the cause is usually excessively wet soil (perhaps because of poor drainage caused by the drainage holes becoming plugged), which crowds out the oxygen needed by roots.

All water used should be at the same temperature as the room. Using warm water in cold weather or in a cold room can damage the roots, especially in winter; the same applies to using cold water in a warm room. A great deal depends on the quality, or rather the composition, of the water. Rainwater is the best of all, or water from a brook, river or pond, but only if it is not polluted with industrial wastes. Tap water is suitable if it does not contain too much chlorine or is not too 'hard'. However, even it may be used if softened or boiled and then allowed to cool.

Because moisture requirements differ so greatly they are given separately under the description for each individual plant.

TEMPERATURE

Temperature is a further important factor influencing a plant's growth. It is very important to know the optimum as well as the maximum and minimum temperatures for growing various plants, especially those from the tropics and subtropics. Temperature requirements vary greatly not only according to the species but also in relation to the stage of the plant's growth and the time of the year. Plants for cool rooms require a winter temperature of about 8 to 12° C. (47 to 54° F.), plants for semi-warm rooms a winter temperature of about 15 to 18° C. (59 to 65° F.), and plants for warm rooms a winter temperature of about 18 to 22° C. (65 to 72° F.). This is only a rough guide corresponding to the conditions found in their natural habitat. The temperature requirements of plants during the year may be shown by a curve on a graph which rises slightly during the winter rest period, reaches its peak from June to August and then gradually drops again to its original starting point. For many plants September or October marks the end of growth and the onset of the dormant period.

Apart from the different temperatures which occur in the course of the year, plants are also affected by the differences in temperature within the daily 24-hour period. The room temperature should never be higher in the evening or at night than during the daytime. The temperature curve during the course of the 24-hour period should correspond to the changes in temperature under natural conditions, i. e. it should rise in the morning and reach its peak around noon, after which it should gradually drop and remain at this low level from evening until sunrise. In conclusion, there are a few basic rules that should be observed if house plants are to be grown with success:

Keep in mind the plant's origin and the conditions of its native habitat.

The room temperature should be regulated according to the season of the year.

The room temperature should correspond to the daily fluctuations of night and day.

THE GROWING MEDIUM

The growing medium is the chief source of a plant's nourishment. It should contain all the nutrients required for healthy growth and much depends on its quality. Plain garden soil can be used but the specially prepared composts which are offered for sale at garden centres and in shops are more suitable. These may be either soil or peat based. The soil-based ones are known as John Innes potting composts Nos. 1, 2 or 3. Each consists of a basic mixture of 7 parts by bulk of loam, 3 parts of peat and 2 parts of coarse sand, and is enriched with fertilizer. The number refers to the quantity of fertilizer present. In general, John Innes potting compost No. 1 is used for slow-growing plants in small pots, John Innes potting compost No. 2 for medium-sized plants, and John Innes potting compost No. 3 for vigorous plants in large containers. For many of the house plants it is advisable to add extra peat to these composts, e. g. 3 parts of ready-mixed compost to 1 part of peat. There is also a John Innes seed-sowing compost.

The peat-based composts are mixtures of peat and sand or peat and vermiculite, again with added fertilizer, and with their good water-retention properties they are ideal growing mediums for many house plants.

In addition to these soil- and peat-based composts some other specialized ready-mixed composts for orchids, cacti, etc. are available at certain places and, of course, you can prepare your own if you wish.

The following are the most important materials for using in home-made composts.

Peat. This contains only a small percentage of inorganic nutrients and is added to soil mixtures to improve the soil structure and regulate its acidity. Its beneficial effect on the growth of roots is also important. Combined with sand it is the best medium for rooting cuttings in propagators.

Peat may be added to soil mixtures for practically all house plants or one of the peat-based composts can be used. It is particularly good for tropical plants which require more acid soil.

Plants can also be grown in peat alone if they are given an occasional light application of liquid feed after they have rooted.

Leafmould. Essentially this consists of decomposed leaves. Well-ripened leafmould is a good medium for most thermophilous plants. Half-decomposed leaves are a good admixture to the compost for orchids, anthuriums, bromeliads and other epiphytic plants.

Rotted turves. This type of loamy soil has a crumb-like structure and the best is obtained from closely cropped turf with roots just below the surface. To make the loam, sections of turf should be lifted up, piled in a heap with the grass side downwards and left to rot for two years, the heap being turned occasionally during this time. At the end of the two-year period they will have disintegrated into a fine crumbly loamy soil.

COMPONENTS ADDED TO GARDEN SOILS

To loosen or lighten the soil for a number of uses various ingredients are combined with the basic constituents.

Sand loosens soil by separating the particles. It is very important that it should be added to humus-rich soils as these, when dry, would otherwise absorb too much water. Apart from this, sand is used primarily in propagators. Coarse sand is best.

Charcoal pieces varying in size from large hailstones

to small nuts are a good addition to epiphytic soil mixtures, e. g. for orchids, anthuriums and bromeliads. They keep the soil healthy in that they absorb excess moisture. Charcoal powder can be sprinkled on the cut surfaces of fleshy cuttings to prevent decay.

Roots of the ferns *Polypodium vulgare* and *Osmunda regalis* are the chief components of mixtures for growing orchids. Before planting, the roots of these ferns should be washed thoroughly and broken up into small pieces.

Although not very easy to obtain, *Sphagnum squarrosum* is important in house plant cultivation where it has a number of uses: dried and torn into bits it forms the second constituent of the mixture for growing orchids; freshly cut tips are used as an outer cover for the rootballs of orchids, anthuriums and bromeliads; when propagating plants by means of air-layering wet sphagnum is wrapped around the cuts to act as a rooting medium. And, no matter what kind of plant, the soil in the pot

MIXTURES SUITABLE FOR ORCHIDS

	Osmunda regalis	*Polypodium vulgare*	*Sphagnum squarrosum*	Loam	Leafmould
Epiphytes	2 parts	2 parts	2 parts	—	1 part
Epiphytes — modern mixture	4 parts	—	2 parts	—	1 part
Terrestrial species	2 parts	2 parts	4 parts	2 parts	—

MIXTURES SUITABLE FOR BROMELIADS

	Half-decomposed leafmould	Rough peat	Charcoal	Coarse sand	Loam
Epiphytes	2 parts	4 parts	1 part	1 part	—
Terrestrial species	—	4 parts	—	1 part	2 parts

can be covered with sphagnum which enhances the appearance and acts as a filter that softens the water reaching the roots. Such a surface layer, however, should be replaced by fresh sphagnum every now and then.

House plants need different types of potting composts and the text accompanying each illustrated species also describes the most appropriate compost to use.

FEEDING

Plants take up food from the soil through their roots and, as the nutrients in the soil are used up within a certain period following repotting, it is important to give regular applications of extra feed. The composition and dosage of the feed, however, is not the same for all plants, it is governed by their age, type, condition, and the time of the year. Young plants require some nutrients, though not in excessive amounts — it is better to give them too little rather than too much. Nitrogen is needed primarily in the first stage of growth, and phosphorus and potassium before the flowering and fruit-bearing period. During the dormant period little, if any, feeding is required. A large plant of rapid growth needs more nutrients than a small, slow-growing plant; so large plants may be given a weekly application of fertilizer, while slower-growing plants, such as anthuriums, bromeliads and camellias, are fed at two-week intervals. As the period of daylight lengthens the life processes quicken, and as light intensity decreases they slow down. Feed should be applied accordingly. Indoors, of course, growth does not cease altogether during the winter months and plants that flower in winter should be given extra feed at this time as well. In conclusion, remember that the rule of thumb for feeding is: feed only during the growing period and only after the plants are well established.

REPOTTING

House plants need repotting if they are not to suffer from lack of food. Often, however, repotting is necessary for other reasons as well, e. g. when the soil in the pot turns sour, when the roots are diseased, etc., and these reasons vary for different plants. Whereas once a year is frequent enough for most, some exhaust the nutrients so rapidly that they have to be repotted several times annually. On the other hand, large, strong specimens of palm, oleander and other house plants need not be moved yearly but only when they show signs of weakening growth. The best way to determine whether or not a plant needs potting on is to tip it out of its pot and inspect the roots — if the pot is full of roots then the plant should be repotted. The best time for this is in spring before growth starts; plants should never be moved during the winter rest period. The compost used for potting should be only slightly moist but the plants themselves should be watered thoroughly before potting on so that the whole root ball is moist. Move plants to pots that are only slightly bigger than the ones they are in because if moved to much larger pots their roots do not grow to fill all the available space and the compost may become sour. With some kinds of plants the roots grow so vigorously that they push the root ball up out of the pot. In such a case trim the bottom roots before putting the plant in the new pot.

The method of repotting is as follows: take up the pot in the left hand, turn it upside down and tip out the plant with root ball intact by knocking the pot lightly against the edge of the table. Carefully loosen the roots with a small wooden peg. New clay flower pots should be submerged in water for several hours before use. Old pots should be scrubbed clean with boiling water. If using a clay pot put some coarse grit or broken crocks in the bottom — this is unnecessary with plastic pots. Then place some of the fresh potting mixture in the base of the pot and stand the plant upright in the middle so that it is neither too high nor too low in the pot. Holding the plant with the left hand fill in the space around the old soil ball with the new potting compost, firming it down with the fingers or a wooden peg so that there are no gaps between the roots. When repotting has been completed give the plant a good watering.

House plants are very sensitive after repotting, so place them in a light spot but not in direct sunlight. For the first ten to fourteen days keep the room temperature at a higher level, ventilate carefully and water sparingly. Some plants, e. g. pelargoniums and fuchsias, can be cut back when repotting is carried out. Use a sharp knife and cut back hard, leaving only short stems on which new shoots will rapidly emerge. In summer such trimmed plants produce many side branches and bear an abundance of flowers. Untrimmed plants are bare at the base and make unsightly specimens. Ficus, dracaena and other species may also be cut back. The sections removed may be used as cuttings if required.

FLOWER POTS

The pots in which house plants are grown need not be of a porous material such as clay. Experience has shown that non-porous pots — porcelain, plastic, or painted — are not only as good but often even better. In clay pots the soil may either dry out too much or else is not sufficiently moist, the reason being that the moisture is not only absorbed by the plant roots but also evaporates through the walls of the pot. Non-porous pots do not have this drawback. It is true that in clay pots the soil is better aerated and the danger of root decay is less but water must be applied more frequently. Non-porous pots must be provided with good drainage and should have an opening at the side or base to allow for the run-off of excess water. If the pot does not have such an opening let the soil soak up the water for about half an hour after watering and then tip the pot on its side to let excess water run off. If the potted plant is to be stood in another non-porous container then drainage material should be placed in the base of this container before standing the pot inside.

In order to select the right size of pot it is necessary

to know what kind of plant is to be put in it and how large that plant may grow. Seedlings or rooted cuttings are naturally put in quite small pots and progressively moved to larger ones as they grow. Plants of vigorous growth that make abundant roots cannot be kept in small pots for long. On the other hand, slow-growing plants and ones with only a few roots should not be grown in large pots as the roots cannot fill the available space, the soil then becomes sour and the plant dies. A wooden tub is useful for really large house plants such as palms, oleanders and the like; the inside should be slightly blackened by burning before putting the plant in, the outside may be painted any colour. To make handling and moving large tubs easier, metal handles may be attached on either side.

DISHES FOR PLACING UNDER POTS

House plants are often placed on furniture which must be protected against water damage by placing the pot containing the plant in an impermeable dish. Any surplus water remaining in the dish after watering should be drained off after an hour or so, otherwise it prevents access of air to the base of the pot and the compost becomes waterlogged; only a few plants do not mind or even need to stand in water all the time, e. g. cyperus. If the dish is deep enough it can be filled with pebbles so that the water which drains through does not touch the base of the pot. Good for a large space, such as a table top, windowsill and the like, is a pan of zinc sheet fitted to the exact size of the area available and with edges turned up about $1\frac{1}{2}$ in. (4 cm.). Paint the outside of the pan so that it blends with the surroundings and fill the bottom with pebbles. Vapour rising around the plant from the water that runs off and remains standing in the pan will continually provide the plant with a mildly moist atmosphere.

Use can be made of the space above a radiator in a similar way, but in this case the pan may be somewhat deeper. Cover the bottom with small pieces of coke or other aggregate and stand the pots on this. Coke gives off a great deal of water vapour and thus the plants continually have a slightly moist atmosphere.

PESTS AND DISEASES

If house plants are not provided with the necessary conditions for growth and development they may easily become diseased and thus more prone to attack by pests. It is, therefore, advisable to be thoroughly acquainted with the conditions required by the given species for healthy growth. The variety of house plants is so great that a suitable kind can be selected for any given environment and, as a great many species have similar requirements, it is possible to have a very diverse collection. As has already been stated the conditions for good growth include the combined effect of several basic factors, namely soil, light, temperature and moisture. Plants should be checked regularly for any signs of disease or attack by pests so that prompt action can be taken or a suitable insecticide or fungicide applied. Diseases may be caused by improper care, physiological disorders, fungi, or may result from damage.

Physiological disorders are caused by unfavourable growing conditions — the adverse effect of too much or too little light, soil, temperature or moisture. Excessive soil moisture or low temperatures are common causes of trouble; sansevieria and fleshy plants may even die as a result. Overwatering causes the leaves to turn yellow, then brown and finally to drop off, a symptom often seen in the rubber tree, *Ficus elastica*. Frequently plants die as a result of careless ventilation on cold winter days; therefore, when airing the room it is recommended to open those windows where there are no plants. A constant draught is likewise detrimental. Many plants make poor growth and die in rooms with coal-gas heating; certain kinds of bromeliads, clivia, sansevieria and chlorophytum will stand up to this if given some ventilation.

The most common fungus disease, caused by *Erysiphales* fungi, is the well known mildew which appears as a whitish furry coating on the leaves of roses, young apple trees and also house plants such as begonias and cinerarias. Plants should be sprayed as a preventive measure, or at the first signs of the disease, with a suitable fungicide.

The most common insect diseases are caused by aphids (greenfly), which are generally found on the soft parts of plants. They suck sap from foliage often causing the leaves to curl. Because aphids multiply very rapidly plants should be sprayed with an insecticide at the first signs. If already markedly affected destroy aphids by putting the insecticide, suitably diluted, in a container, holding the plant upside down and washing the top parts in the solution.

Spider mites, commonly called red spiders, attack practically all plants, even ones with leaves as stiff as those of ficus and aspidistra. They occur on the underside of leaves and suck the sap, causing the attacked leaves to turn brown and die. Preventive measures include repeated spraying and, if possible, immersion of the plant top in an insecticidal solution. These pests are more likely to be a problem in a hot dry atmosphere.

Woolly aphids, with their hair-like waxy covering, attack certain plants such as clivia, croton, coffea, cacti and succulents. The bodies of these insects are red but this is evident only when they are crushed for otherwise they look like tufts of cottonwool. Woolly aphids should be removed with a brush dipped in alcohol and the plants then sprayed with a proprietary solution. Spraying should be repeated if the aphids show up again.

Scale insects are harmful homopterous insects that multiply very rapidly. Insecticides are most effective if used in spring before the insects have acquired their thick scale-like armour. Later they must be scraped off with a wooden stick and the plant sprayed as a further preventive measure.

A word of warning: when using any kind of chemical preparation it is extremely important to follow carefully the manufacturer's instructions. Many insecticides are poisonous to fish and warm-blooded animals (including human beings) and should not be used in the home; so make sure you obtain one of the preparations recommended for use on house plants and keep it out of the reach of children and pets.

CLEANING LEAVES

Even the cleanest room is not without dust. This settles on plant leaves and prevents the proper functioning of the life processes vital to the plant's growth, namely transpiration, evaporation and photosynthesis. It is, therefore, necessary to sponge the leaves occasionally with a soft sponge dipped in lukewarm water, which should be exchanged several times during the process. Support the leaf with the hand and sponge from the base to the tip. At the same time inspect for any signs of disease. Plants with tougher leaves, such as ficus, philodendron, aspidistra and the like, may also be given an overhead spraying or stood out in the rain in summer.

PROPAGATION

It is very interesting to propagate house plants, and those that we have propagated ourselves give us far greater pleasure than ones purchased in a shop.

Annuals are generally multiplied by means of seeds. Most perennials, on the other hand, cannot always be grown from seed as these are sometimes sterile or difficult to germinate. A further problem lies in the fact that many plants do not come true from seed — they may not inherit the special characteristics of the parent plant — for example, the offspring of most plants with variegated foliage have green leaves.

Vegetative propagation by means of parts of the plant ensures that the offspring will have most of the characteristics of the parent. It is important that the plants used for this method of propagation are healthy and possess all the desired qualities. The commonest method of vegetative propagation is by cuttings, which are taken usually in spring and sometimes also in the summer. To root cuttings properly it is necessary to have a small propagator. This can be purchased, or it is possible to make use of a glass case or an aquarium, or even a pot covered with a glass jar or plastic bag. The size of the propagator depends on the number of plants you wish to propagate.

You may wish to install an automatically controlled heating system in the bottom of the propagator and

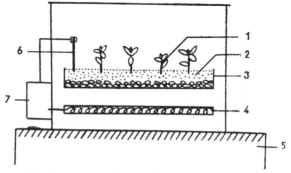

Fig. 1. Metal aquarium of larger dimensions used as a propagator
1. cuttings 2. rooting medium 3. metal dish 4. electric heating
5. stand 6. contact thermometer 7. relay

one way of doing this is to use a tube about ½ in. (1 cm.) in diameter into which a spiral of resistance wire covered with ceramic insulating rings is inserted. The outlets must also be insulated. The temperature is regulated by means of a contact thermometer. Electric heating, of course, must be installed by an expert for incorrect installation might be a source of injury. About 2 in. (5 cm.) above the heating element place a pan of rust-proof metal sheet with upturned edges and on this a ¾-in. (2-cm.) thick layer of pebbles topped by a 2½-in. (6-cm.) layer of the growing medium. The cuttings of some plants require a temperature of 25 to 28° C. (77 to 83° F.) e. g. *Ficus elastica*, codiaeum and dieffenbachia. Others, e. g. abutilon, various begonias, hibiscus, hydrangea, impatiens, fuchsia and pelargonium, require a temperature of 18 to 20° C. (65 to 68° F.).

Another type of propagator consists of an electric light bulb placed under an inverted flowerpot on which is stood a dish of water containing a smaller dish with the growing medium. The latter is then covered with a large glass jar.

Cuttings strike best in an environment with constant moisture and good ventilation. For rapid rooting air must have access to the cut surface and for this reason cuttings are sometimes inserted at a slant into sand which is used to fill the space between two clay flowerpots of different sizes placed one inside the other. The bottom of the larger pot is covered with drainage material, the smaller, porous pot is stoppered and filled to about one-fifth its depth with water. Water capillarity plus strong surface evaporation keep the sand layer moist. That this is a method not to be underestimated is evident

Fig. 2. Propagator heated by a bulb
1. bell glass or glass jar 2. cuttings 3. dish with rooting medium
4. dish with water 5. bulb 6. inverted flower pot 7. stand

Fig. 3.   Cuttings under a glass
Fig. 4.   Cuttings inserted round the sides of the pot strike well and rapidly

from the fact that the young roots are formed mostly in the sand next to the sides of the inner pot to which they remain tightly pressed. Another similar method is to place a smaller flowerpot upside down inside a larger one which has been provided with good drainage at the bottom. The space between the two is filled with sand and the cuttings inserted round the edges of the two pots with the cut surfaces pressed to the sides of the pots. In this way plenty of air is supplied to the cuts and the cuttings thus root rapidly. In both the above instances the pots with the cuttings are covered with a glass jar or large plastic bag.

THE ROOTING MEDIUM

Cuttings root best in coarse sand. A mixture of peat and sand in equal parts is also very good, as peat stimulates the growth of roots and forms a ball around the roots that holds together when the cuttings are being potted up, thereby making it easier for them to become established. Some cuttings, for example those of pelargonium and tradescantia, are put directly into small pots in sandy soil. The propagator as well as dishes and pots should be washed out well with hot water before putting in the rooting medium in order to destroy any disease germs that may be present. Insert the cuttings to a depth of about 1 in. (2 cm.) and press them in with the fingers. When they have all been inserted water them well and then cover the propagating case with a sheet of glass, or in the case of a dish or pot use an inverted glass jar or plastic bag. In sunny weather spray the cuttings to keep them from wilting.

A good method, already described, is to immerse the pot or container with the cuttings in a bowl of water; this does away with the need for watering as the water in the bowl is distributed by capillary action throughout the cutting medium keeping it continually moist.

Keep the propagator covered with glass until the cuttings begin to make roots. Then ventilate gradually to harden them off. When the cuttings are well rooted pot each one up separately and put them in a warm situation. Water them frequently to prevent wilting.

PROPAGATION BY CUTTINGS

A cutting is a piece of stem, root or leaf that, given the proper conditions, will form roots of its own and develop into an independent plant. The different kinds of cuttings are: green soft-stem cuttings, leaf cuttings, hard-stem cuttings, and root cuttings.

Soft-stem cuttings. These are taken from annual shoots; rapid healing of the wound and the formation of a callus are very important for the making of roots. The cuttings should be $2\frac{1}{2}$ to 3 in. (6 to 8 cm.) long and those taken from the side of older shoots root better and more rapidly. In the case of some plants, such as ficus, dieffenbachia, codiaeum, etc., it is better to take longer cuttings with four or five leaves, and in order to

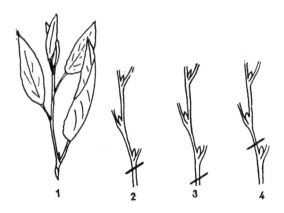

Fig. 5. Stem cutting
1. before treatment   2. correctly cut   3. cut too low   4. cut too high

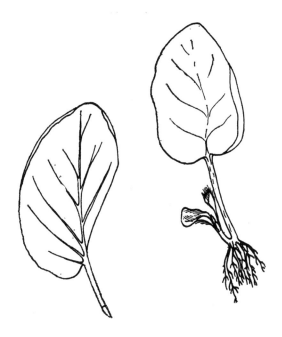

Fig. 6.   Leaf cutting of saintpaulia

make the most of the space in the propagator the leaves
can be rolled up and bound. To prevent the cuttings
from being uprooted tie each to a thin stake. The cuttings
should be taken and inserted in the rooting medium as
quickly as possible to prevent the wound from drying
out, for they root poorly if wilted. Only in the case of
cacti and succulents are the cuttings left to dry before
insertion. The cuttings of plants that exude a milky
white or yellow sap, e. g. ficus and euphorbia, should
be inserted in dry sand with the cut side down. When

the cut has dried wash the sand off and insert the cuttings in the usual rooting medium. To keep cuttings from wilting through excessive evaporation, the leaf blades of some species should be shortened by about one-third. To promote more rapid rooting dust the cut with a hormone-rooting powder.

Rooting in water. Some plants root better in water than in sand, e. g. *Nerium oleander, Cyperus alternifolius* and sparmannia. Insert the cut end of the prepared cutting in a bottle of water and anchor with a wad of cottonwool. Change the water once a week. This method may be used at any time of the year though it is best done in spring or summer.

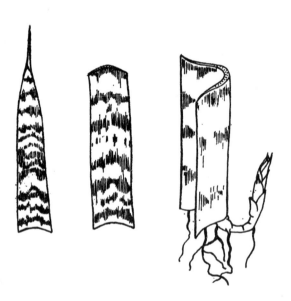

Fig. 7. Leaf cutting of sansevieria

Leaf cuttings. The leaves of most plants are capable of forming roots but not all form buds from which a new plant will grow. In the case of ficus, aucuba and hedera the leaf stalk will make roots and the leaf will last four to six years but it will never develop into a new plant. For purposes of propagation rooting the leaves of such plants is, therefore, useless. Only species that have adventitious buds on the blade and leaf stalk can be multiplied by leaf cuttings, e. g. *Begonia rex,* which forms adventitious buds on the whole surface of the blade as well as along the length of the stalk. The strongest plants are obtained from the bud located at the junction of the blade and leaf stalk. Various kinds of saintpaulia, peperomia, *Cyperus alternifolius,* sansevieria, and all fleshy-leaved plants such as echeveria, kalanchoë and crassula are propagated by leaf cuttings. The strongest plants are obtained by inserting the whole leaf, with $\frac{1}{2}$ to $\frac{3}{4}$ in. (1 or 2 cm.) of leaf stalk attached. Sansevieria is propagated by cutting the leaves diagonally into $2\frac{1}{2}$- to 3-in. (6-to 8-cm.)-long sections. The conditions necessary for the rooting of leaf cuttings are the same as for soft-stem cuttings.

Some plants form buds on the leaf margins, e. g. certain species of *Bryophyllum, Asplenium viviparum,* etc. and these can be propagated by placing the leaf on the surface of the rooting medium and covering the pot with an inverted glass jar or plastic bag. The margins of the leaves will soon form plants which should be potted up separately when they are rooted.

Hard-stem cuttings. Many plants develop hard stems, or trunks, relatively early in their lives and the lower leaves gradually fall off, leaving a scar with a visible bud embryo which, under certain conditions, may develop into a new plant. This property is displayed by some species of the genera *Dieffenbachia, Monstera, Philodendron, Dracaena* and *Cordyline.* When the plant is too

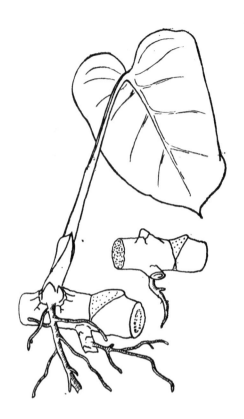

Fig. 8.   Hard-stem cutting of philodendron

old or ungainly the top part with green foliage can be cut off and potted up — a useful method with monstera and philodendron. Cut the remainder of the stem into sections with one bud each, dust the cuts with charcoal powder and place them on the surface of the rooting medium in the propagator. They will soon form roots and new plants will grow from the buds. Pot up the rooted cuttings. Some kinds form new growth on stolons, e. g. *Saxifraga stolonifera*, or on flower stems, e. g. phalangium. In such cases propagation is very simple: when large enough the new growths are simply removed and potted up.

PROPAGATION BY DIVISION

This is the simplest method of propagation and one that is frequently used. Spring is the usual time for multiplying house plants by this means. If the parent

Fig. 9.   Propagation by division of clumps

plants are given favourable conditions for growth they soon form large clumps and often the centre of these clumps deteriorates and after a time dies. In such a case it is necessary to divide the plant into several smaller clumps. Some clumps can easily be separated simply by pulling them apart, others have to be divided with a long sharp knife. Pot up the separated clumps into suitably sized pots, preferably smaller rather than larger ones. Species of *Aspidistra, Asparagus, Calla, Cyperus, Isolepis, Clivia, Acorus, Ophiopogon* and *Sansevieria* are propagated by this method. Sansevierias with yellow-edged leaves retain their variegated foliage only if increased by division; if propagated by leaf cuttings the new plants usually have completely green foliage.

AIR-LAYERING

This method of propagation is used when a propagator is not available or if there are any doubts about the severed plant section forming roots. It is a good method for plants with tall stems such as ficus, dracaena and the like. At the point where you want the plant to form roots make a cut upwards at a strong angle at least two-thirds across the stem, and insert a match to keep the cut open. Dust the cut with a hormone rooting powder and fill in the space with damp moss, sphagnum if possible, moulding it also around the cut. Then wrap a piece of plastic around the moss, binding it at the top and bottom, to ensure that the moss remains moist. To prevent the plant top from breaking off tie it to a stake above and below the wad of moss. When well-developed roots appear, which takes four to five weeks, remove the plastic, cut off the top and pot it up together with the moss packing.

WHERE TO PUT HOUSE PLANTS

When growing house plants it is very important that they should be placed in a suitable spot. As has already been pointed out plants are living objects and must be provided with the conditions they require for good growth. Many plants purchased in the shop soon die simply because their temperature, moisture and light requirements have been neglected. Therefore, so as not to be disappointed with the results, you should find out the conditions of the plant's native habitat when purchasing a new kind and adapt the conditions at home accordingly. However, as it is not always possible to provide the special environment required by a particular plant it is really best to select those that will thrive in the available conditions. Fortunately the choice of plants is so wide that it is possible to find a suitable species for practically any situation.

Plants that grow in the humid tropical rain forests have practically no rest period. If such plants are to be grown indoors they must be provided with warmth and moisture throughout the year. In tropical jungles plants grow at various levels and this must be kept in mind when selecting a suitable spot for them indoors. Plants growing naturally at the lowest level need very shaded conditions. These include aglaonema, certain species of *Anthurium, Fittonia, Maranta, Philodendron,* xerophilous species of *Paphiopedilum,* numerous ferns, selaginella, etc. Plants that grow in the tree tops are platycerium and nepenthes, of the bromeliads vriesea, nidularium and guzmania, and of the orchids phalaenopsis. True jewels of the tropics, they can be grown with success even in the home if given conditions as much like their native habitat as possible, in a closed window glasshouse or in a plant case placed by a window. Both must be heated, best of all by some form of electrical heating which can be regulated, and the plants should be placed inside in the same arrangement as in their native habitat, in other words those that grow on the ground should be put at the bottom of the container and those that grow in tree tops should be suspended above. Only plants with the same requirements and ones that are found growing together in their native habitat should be put in the same container. In winter the temperature in such a glasshouse must be kept at 20° C. (68° F.) in the daytime and 18° C. (65° F.) at night; a slightly

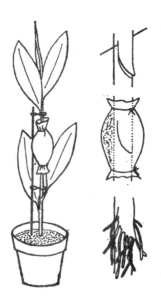

Fig. 10. Air-layering — rooting direct on the plant into moss packing

higher temperature is better. The soil and atmospheric moisture are governed by the temperature as well; at lower temperatures plants need less moisture. During the growth period in summer the temperature in an enclosed glass case may rise to 30 °C. (86° F.) if suitably shaded. In the event of long spells of cold and rainy weather in summer the case may be heated slightly even at this time.

However, some plants, native to the damp tropical jungles, have become entirely acclimatized to the conditions prevailing in rooms. They are dieffenbachia, aglaonema, anthurium and certain kinds of philodendron. These may be grown by a closed window in summer but must be shielded from the mid-day sun. The treatment is different for plants that are from periodically dry regions where the warm, damp season corresponds to summer in our part of the world, whereas winter in such regions is a period of drought. Found here are many plants of the families *Orchidaceae, Bromeliaceae,* and others that are widely grown in Europe. Plants from these regions must be given a rest period, otherwise they flower poorly or not at all. *Dendrobium nobile* and its many hybrids come from these periodically dry regions and require warmth and moisture during the growing season. In September water should be withheld and the temperature lowered. The bulbs are kept at this cooler temperature in dry surroundings until February, when buds begin to form on leafless two-year-old bulbs. At this time watering should be resumed and the temperature raised. The plants will bear an abundance of flowers within six weeks. If these orchids are kept continually in a warm, moist environment without any lowering of the temperature and limiting of the water they will make growth but will never produce flowers.

Plants from periodically dry regions should be placed by a slightly shaded window in summer and in full sunlight in winter. The winter temperature should be between 10 and 18° C. (50 to 65° F.), depending on the species.

Other plants grow in deserts or semi-deserts, e. g. cacti and succulents. These should be given a poorer soil, placed in a sunny, well-ventilated spot and watered sparingly. The winter temperature should be kept at 10 to 12° C. (50 to 54° F.).

Plants from the subtropics, such as agave, acacia, aucuba, laurus, myrtus, rosmarinus, etc., are grown out of doors in summer and moved indoors for the winter, where they are kept in a cool room at a temperature of 5 to 10° C. (41 to 50° F.).

Many lovely ornamental plants can be grown successfully in rooms without any special equipment. The best place, naturally, is by the window. If the windowsill is not wide enough this can be solved by using a wider board supported by another narrower board or two broader laths attached to the room-side edge. The boards can be painted an attractive colour. It is better for plant roots if the pots stand on a wooden board rather than on a stone wall. A particularly good method is to put an asbestos or wooden box lined with metal or plastic beside or just under the window, fill it with peat or moss and into this plunge the pots with the plants. This keeps the plants from drying out and promotes good growth. It would be ideal if, when building a house, the plans included a brick or concrete trough inside under the window which could be filled with peat and used in the way just described. In a small flat plants may be put in larger ornamental containers and the space between the pot and container filled with moss or peat. It is important, however, as has already been pointed out, to provide good drainage by putting pebbles or broken crocks in the bottom of the ornamental container so that the pot does not stand in water. In this case it is not necessary to put a dish under the pot. In rooms with large windows plants may be put in various places and not just by the window. However, they must have sufficient light, and this is determined by many different factors, e. g. the size of the window, the distance from the window, the thickness of the curtains, the colour of the walls — whether light or dark — etc. If plants cannot be placed right beside the window they may be arranged on a low table in front of it. In this case it is recommended to put thick glass or some other protective cover on the tabletop. Such tables or plant stands when placed some distance from the window are good only for larger and lighter rooms. Stands crowded with plants are not attractive, it is far better if they hold only a few well-formed specimens. Larger specimens of ficus, palm, philodendron and the like are better grown as solitary subjects. Remember, however, to place them in a spot with sufficient light.

WINDOW GLASSHOUSE:
A — built-in container 18 to 28 in. (45 to 70 cm.) wide   B — drainage outlet for run-off of surplus water   C — outer double glass wall   D — inner, sliding, glass wall   E — shading   F — summer ventilation   G — winter ventilation   H — air vent closure   I — illumination   K — grid for epiphytes   L — layer of drainage material, pebbles or crocks   M — sand   N — peat   O — electrical heating   P — regulation of soil temperature   R — thermostat   S — moisture content indicator

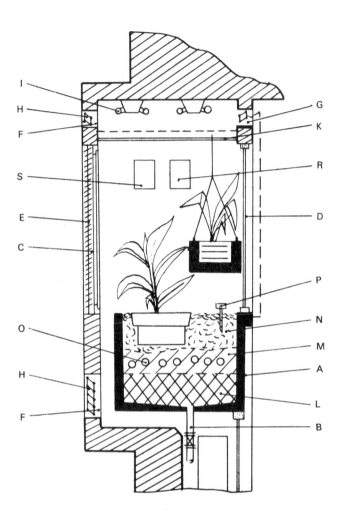

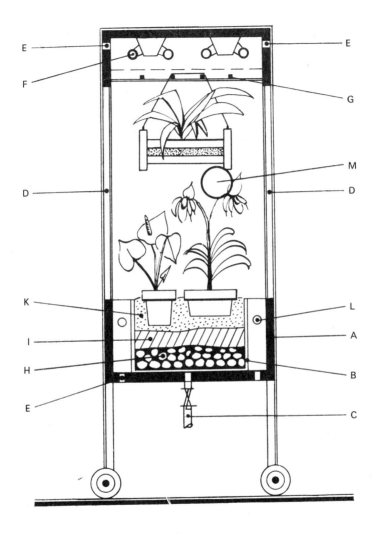

WINDOW GLASSHOUSES AND PLANT CASES

Many species of plants that grow in damp tropical jungles in the wild can be cultivated in a window glasshouse or plant case, above all certain orchids and bromeliads, certain ferns, aglaonema, anthurium (small species), *Ficus repens,* nepenthes, philodendron and platycerium. Larger pots are stood in the container at the bottom of the case and surrounded by moss. On the sides can be hung epiphytic plants that grow on other plants in their native habitat but are not parasites. These may be attached to a piece of cork or put in a small basket. A very attractive effect may be obtained by growing epiphytic plants on a branch or log. For this purpose select a crooked branch of hard wood with thick, cracked bark, e. g. pear tree. For larger plants it is necessary to bore a hole with a drainage outlet. For an attractive arrangement put larger plants at the base and smaller ones at the top. Plants selected for growing in this manner should be tipped out of their pots, the soil removed from the roots and the latter wrapped in fibre. Thus prepared they can be inserted in the bored-out holes. A good general rule to follow is to put large plants on large branches and only small ones on thin branches.

INDOOR GLASS CASE:
A — outer container up to 24 in. (60 cm.) wide   B — inside container for plants   C — drainage outlet for run-off of surplus water   D — sliding glass panels   E — ventilation   F — illumination   G — grid for epiphytes   H — layer of drainage material, pebbles or crocks   I — sand   K — peat   L — electrical heating regulated by a thermostat   M — moisture content indicator

HOUSE PLANTS AND HOLIDAYS

Many people do not grow house plants simply because they don't know what to do with them when they are away for a long period. A three- or four-week holiday, however, is no reason for foregoing the year-round pleasure of growing house plants. There are many ways for plants to survive a period without watering. One is to plunge the pots in a box, trough or larger pot filled with moist peat or moss which is then watered thoroughly. The important thing is that the container with the plants should be put in a spot with sufficient light for photosynthesis. A good place is a balcony with a western or northern exposure.

HOUSE PLANTS IN SUMMER

If plants can be placed out of doors on a balcony or in the garden in the summer months it is always better than if they remain in the room throughout the year. Plants put out of doors in summer benefit not only from the fresh air but also from being watered by rain. Much, however, depends on when the plants are put out and where — in the sun or shade. The best time for moving plants is in mid-June when the temperature is more or less stable. The change must not be too abrupt. All plants, be they fond of sun or shade, should first be put in the shade, best of all under a tree, and after fourteen days moved to their permanent summer site. Sun-loving plants should be put in a sunny position, shade-loving plants should be left in the shade of a tree. The pots should be plunged in the ground so that the compost does not dry out too rapidly. If only a few plants are being moved out of doors then these may be plunged into sand or peat in a box placed on a balcony or patio. If there is no available shade in the garden a simple construction can be made to provide it. Measure out a square or rectangular space, put a strong stake in each corner, lay two laths across the stakes and then a cover of reeds or small boards. Larger plants should be staked so that they are not overturned by strong winds. Plants should be inspected every evening and watered if they are dry. They will also appreciate being sprayed over with water during the day in hot, dry weather. If a plant is making too vigorous growth take up the pot and check that the roots are not growing out into the surrounding soil. If they are, cut them off and plunge the pot back in the ground. In the summer months, when house plants are in full growth, they may be given additional feed in liquid form as described in the chapter on feeding. In mid-September, or at the latest the end of the month, house plants should be taken back indoors for the winter. Before doing so, clean the plants and wash the leaves with water, using a sponge or cloth for the purpose. Remove dry and yellow leaves and snip off dried tips. Then spray the plants with a proprietary insecticide several times to make certain all pests are destroyed. After the plants have been moved indoors air the room frequently and acclimatize them to their new environment.

WALL DECORATION

House plants are also very attractive as wall decoration, this being an extremely practical method of growing them, especially in small flats where every bit of space counts. Here, more than in any other instance, however, it is necessary to keep the decoration simple and practical. Hanging raffia or wicker baskets or pottery vessels are very effective, and if you want more than just the trailing, pendent arrangement and would like the plant to cover the wall upwards and to the sides, a good solution is to attach a thin bamboo lattice to the wall to which shoots can be tied. Good plants for such hanging containers are tradescantia, callisia, scindapsus, hedera, oplismenus, hoya, piper and *Philodendron scandens,* all green foliage plants. To keep the baskets from getting soiled when watering it is recommended to enclose the plant's pot in a plastic bag before it goes into the basket. Plants should be of small dimensions and potted up in small pots.

HOUSE PLANTS IN ORNAMENTAL BOWLS AND DISHES

Some plants are more attractive when positioned with other plants than when standing by themselves. Besides this, there is often not enough space in a room to put out several pots of solitary specimens. In both instances the problem is easily solved by the use of ornamental flower bowls and dishes containing several different kinds of plants. Those that are sold at the florist's and purchased as gifts for various occasions serve only a short-term purpose. Home growers, however, are interested in having such containers as a permanent ornament in their homes, with the plants lasting as long as possible. The bowls may be of various shapes and sizes as well as of different materials. For small plants it is best to use shallow dishes and the selection should consist of such kinds as are found together in the wild and thus have the same characteristics and requirements. It is almost impossible to go wrong if one combines various sorts of plants from the same family, e. g. various species of *Philodendron* with members of the genus *Scindapsus*, various species of *Billbergia* and *Vriesea* with members of the genus *Cryptanthus* and various succulents with cacti. In the case of ceramic bowls that do not have a drainage outlet it is necessary to cover the bottom with a layer of drainage material (pebbles or other aggregate) before inserting the plants. Plants may be put in the ornamental container in their pots and the space filled with moss; alternatively the plants may be tipped out of their pots and inserted in the container in a suitable soil mixture. In the latter case the plants should be grown on in small pots so that the root balls hold together when they are moved.

It is plants with variegated foliage that are generally used for permanent decoration in ornamental bowls. Plants should be inserted in the bowl so that it is evenly filled and the general effect is one of lightness. Taller plants should be placed in the centre, low and trailing plants by the edge. Take care that trailing plants do not entirely conceal the container. The arrangement may be made more striking by adding pieces of bark, oddly shaped twigs, roots and moss-covered stones. Spring or summer is a good time for planting such bowls for then the plants have time to become established before the winter. If plants are inserted in the pots in which they are grown then such ornamental containers may be made up at any time of the year.

PLATES

Abutilon MILL.   *Malvaceae*
Indian Mallow, Flowering Maple,
Lantern Flower

Abutilons are evergreen shrubs with palmate, heart-shaped leaves which are green or brightly mottled. There are about 100 different species, native to the tropics and subtropics. Most widely distributed is *Abutilon hybridum*, produced by the crossing of South American species. Its variously coloured blossoms are borne in winter and summer. It is grown from seed with comparative ease but the seedlings always differ in colour from the parent plant and if you wish to grow seedlings of a given colour then propagation must be carried out by vegetative means. Cuttings may be taken from older plants in spring or summer. All buds and blossoms should be removed from the tip cuttings, which should be 2½ to 3 in. (6 to 8 cm.) long, so that they will root more readily. They should be inserted in pots filled with sand and placed in a propagator or covered with a plastic bag or glass jar and put in a warm, well-lit place. The cuttings will root within three weeks, after which they should be transferred individually to small pots and later potted on into larger pots.

In summer abutilon may be put next to an open window or, better still, on a balcony or out in the garden. At this time it requires abundant watering and an occasional application of liquid feed. It should be taken indoors again before the first frost. It will flower throughout the winter if kept in a well-lit spot at a temperature of 12 to 14° C. (54 to 58° F.). It may be wintered at a lower temperature, but then it will not flower. Older plants should be cut back in spring and transferred to a sandy compost.

Abutilon-Hybrid

48

Acacia MILL.
Mimosa, Wattle

Acacias number more than 500 species, mostly native to Australia. The cut flowering branches from Italy and France are incorrectly called fragrant mimosa. This, however, is the so-called 'sensitive plant', a shrub with leaves that droop if touched, whereas the true acacias are trees or shrubs that are not sensitive to the touch.

Most commonly grown as a house plant is the dwarf species *Acacia armata*, which is of upright, thickly branching habit with small, dark green leaves, ½ to ¾ in. (1 to 2 cm.) long, resembling myrtle. It grows to a height of 2½ ft. (70 cm.). The buds are visible in autumn and the plant is covered with a great profusion of single yellow blossoms in spring. Old plants should be transplanted in May and pruned after they have finished flowering. The annual shoots that are cut off are trimmed to a length of 2¾ in. (7 cm.) and inserted around the sides of a pot in a mixture of equal parts of peat and sand, and covered with a glass jar or plastic bag. At a temperature of 16 to 18° C. (60 to 65° F.) they will root within one month. Rooted cuttings are potted up into 3-in. (8-cm.) pots in a mixture of two parts of peat and one part each of loam and sand (or John Innes or a peat-based compost) and put by a closed window. When the young plants are well rooted the tips should be removed to induce branching. Water should be applied more liberally during the growth period. In July the plants should be potted on into 3½-in. (9-cm.) pots. During the summer they should be placed in an open window in full sunlight, on a balcony, or in the garden. Acacias should be kept in a cool place — 4 to 9° C. (39 to 48° F.) in winter — and watered less frequently.

Acacia armata R. BR. (Syn. *A. paradoxa* DC.)

Achimenes PERS.

Hot Water Plant

The persistent, scaly tubers of these lovely plants produce annual shoots bearing longish, lanceolate leaves with serrated margins. The long, funnel-shaped flowers, opening wide at the mouth, are borne singly. Practically all the species of this genus are natives of Central America. Hybrids of the various species are all classed under the name *Achimenes*-Hybrid.

Propagation is mainly by division of the scaly tubers. In March, tip out the contents of the pots and carefully remove the tubers from the dry soil. Lengthier tubers may be divided up into several parts. Put crocks in the bottom of the pot for drainage and then fill it to within about ¾ in. (2 cm.) of the rim with a mixture of four parts leafmould, two parts peat, two parts rotted turves and one part sand. John Innes or a peat-based compost may also be used. Place the tubers on the surface, five to eight to a 5-in. (13-cm.) pot, and cover them with a ½-in. (1-cm.) layer of compost. At first they need to be kept in shade at a temperature of 18 to 20° C. (65 to 68° F.). When they have sprouted they should be put in a light spot near a window and during the growing period given liquid feed at two-week intervals.

In summer achimenes are best kept near an open window with a northern exposure, where they will flower throughout the season. During the flowering period they should be watered liberally. After flowering is finished water is no longer applied and the plants shed their leaves. When they have dried off they should be stored for the winter in their pots in a room that need not be light but where the temperature is between 10 to 12° C. (50 to 54° F.). In spring the method of cultivation already described is repeated.

Achimenes-Hybrid

Acorus L. *Araceae*
Sweet Flag

Of these bog or water plants with creeping stems and grass-like leaves the best species for growing indoors is *Acorus gramineus* and its two forms: *albivariegatus* with white-striped leaves, and 'Aurei-variegatus' with yellow-striped leaves. Both have narrow leaves and grow to a height of about 8 in. (20 cm.). The flower stem is 6 to 8 in. (15 to 20 cm.) high and the spathe is coloured yellowish green. They are native to Japan. An even smaller species is *A. pusillus*.

In spring the plants can be easily divided into a great many clumps which are planted separately in small pots in a mixture of loam and peat. *A. gramineus* requires a cool room and even when put out in summer it should be provided with partial shade. Because of its decorative foliage it is good for planting in containers with other plants of similar requirements. In summer it thrives out of doors in semi-shade and given a suitable protective covering in the autumn it may even be left out of doors for the winter. Indoors it requires cool temperatures in winter, 4 to 10° C. (39 to 50° F.), and semi-shade. To prevent the roots from drying out stand the plant in a dish of water and replenish this as necessary. Acorus is good as an edging plant for pools with other bog plants. It may also be grown in an aquarium as well as in a terrarium.

Acorus gramineus 'Aureivariegatus'

Aechmea RUIZ & PAV.
Air Pine

Bromeliaceae

There are about 150 known species of the genus *Aechmea,* some of which are epiphytic while others are terrestrial. They originate from Mexico, the West Indies and South America. They are bromeliads with stiff rosettes of serrated leaves and flowers which are borne in spikes, clusters or panicles. Many are cultivated as regularly flowering house plants.

The most commonly grown is *Aechmea fasciata,* which bears flowers from summer until spring. It then forms four to five offsets which should be allowed to grow until they are well rooted. Repot aechmea in spring into a mixture of two parts leafmould, two parts peat and one part sand, or into a peat-based compost. At this time the young, rooted offshoots can be separated from the parent plant and put in smaller pots. Larger species such as *A. fasciata* are grown as solitary specimens in individual pots, less robust species such as *A. racinae* on boughs or in hanging baskets. Indoors they should be placed in a very light position. They are tolerant of a dry atmosphere and therefore extremely suitable for homes with central heating. In winter they will be content with a temperature of about 15° C. (59° F.) if watered sparingly. However, they are also tolerant of higher temperatures, in which case water must be supplied more frequently.

Aechmea fasciata BAK.

Aglaonema SCHOTT.
Poison Dart

Araceae

The genus *Aglaonema* includes lovely decorative herbaceous plants with stout stems that turn woody in time. The leaves are oblong and variegated, the fruits attractive red berries. In some species the leaves grow at the base of the plant, in others they may be as much as 20 in. (50 cm.) high. There are about 40 species, all native to Indonesia. The most brightly variegated is *Aglaonema commutatum* 'Treubii'.

Aglaonemas are terrestrial plants growing in evergreen rain forests but they adapt well to house plant cultivation. Propagation is by stem cuttings taken from the tip, as well as by seed, and is best carried out in spring. Cut off the tips of older plants (there should be four leaves on each cutting) and put them in small pots in a mixture of peat and sand. The pots should be kept in a warm place, best of all in a propagator or window glasshouse. The cuttings will root within a month at a temperature of 22 to 25° C. (72 to 77° F.). The parent plants from which the tips have been removed will soon put out new leaves and will again form attractive specimens in no time at all. When the cuttings have taken root they should be moved to 4-in. (10-cm.) pots filled with a mixture of two parts leafmould, two parts peat and one part sand (or John Innes or a peat-based compost) and the repotted plants should be put in a warm place. If they are grown as solitary specimens aglaonemas must be kept away from the window as they do not thrive in direct sunlight. From March till July liquid feed should be applied at two-week intervals. In winter the temperature should not drop below 15° C. (59° F.). Aglaonemas are repotted in March.

Aglaonema commutatum SCHOTT. 'Treubii'

Ananas MILL.
Pineapple

Bromeliaceae

This small genus comprises five closely related species that are often taken as one. They originate from central Brazil where they still grow wild. Since days of old they have been grown for their delicious fruit in practically all tropical countries in about a hundred cultivated forms.

Best suited as a house plant is *Ananas comosus* 'Variegatus', which is very decorative with its variegated, pale green leaves striped red and white on the margins. The fruit of *A. comosus* is sold on the market. The easiest method of producing young plants for growing indoors is to grow on the tops of fruits purchased in a shop. Pineapple is propagated solely by vegetative means, either by division of offsets growing at the base of the plant, or, as has already been said, by means of the tufts growing at the top of the fruit. The separated plants should be put in sand in a warm propagator where they will take root within six weeks, after which they should be moved to 4-in. (10-cm.) pots containing a mixture of two parts undecayed beech leaves, two parts rough peat, one part loam and one part sand, or John Innes potting compost with an equal amount of peat. At first they must be kept in a warm place and after they have become firmly rooted they should be moved to larger pots. During the growing period water containing diluted feed should be applied sparingly. In winter the best temperature is about 15° C. (59° F.) and watering should be limited.

Ananas comosus MERR. 'Variegatus'

Anthurium SCHOTT.
Flamingo Plant

The thick stem of this upright plant sometimes forms a small trunk. The leaves are heart-shaped or longish lanceolate. Some species are noted for the beauty of their leaves, others for the strikingly coloured bracts. More than 500 species are known to grow in tropical America.

Best suited for cultivation as a house plant is *Anthurium scherzerianum*, which grows to a height of 12 to 16 in. (30 to 40 cm.). The leaves are dark green, lanceolate, 6 to 12 in. (15 to 30 cm.) long and $2\frac{1}{4}$ to 4 in. (6 to 10 cm.) across. The inflorescence consists of flowers arranged in a dense spiral on a thick stem enclosed by a flat, scarlet, pink or white bract, which is erroneously believed to be the flower. The flowers and bracts are long lived.

Indoors the flamingo plant should be put in a light spot beside a closed window but not exposed to full sunlight. During the dormant period in winter the temperature should be kept at a minimum of 16° C. (60° F.) and water should be applied sparingly. In summer the plants should be watered more frequently and liquid feed occasionally applied. In spring, when it has finished flowering, the plant should be transferred to a loose soil mixture consisting of two parts pine leafmould, two parts peat and one part sand, or John Innes potting compost with extra peat or fibre. The pot should be provided with good drainage so that the water can run off. Some species that climb will put out ample roots if provided with a moss-covered stake. Plants are generally propagated by division when they are being replanted. Spots on the leaves should be treated with a fungicide.

Anthurium scherzerianum SCHOTT.

Aphelandra R. BR.

Acanthaceae

This is an herbaceous plant or shrub with opposite (sometimes alternate) leaves and flowers coloured yellow, orange or red. The bracts are variegated and larger than the flowers. There are 60 known species, all native to tropical America. Best known is *Aphelandra squarrosa louisae,* a shrubby, herbaceous plant up to 14 in. (35 cm.) high and native to Brazil. The stems are reddish, the leaves oblong and zebra striped, the bracts lemon-yellow and the flowers dark yellow. Propagation is by leaf cuttings taken in spring and summer but the leaf blades should not be shortened when preparing the cuttings as this would mar the appearance of the plants. The cuttings should be put in a pot in a mixture of sand and peat and placed in a propagator with bottom heat. Rooted cuttings should be moved to 3-in. (8-cm.) pots containing a mixture of four parts leafmould, three parts peat and one part sand (or John Innes or a peat-based compost) and placed by a closed window where they can be shielded from the mid-day sun. In summer the plants should again be transferred to larger pots. Older plants are repotted two or three months after flowering has finished. In winter aphelandra requires a light position, a temperature of 18 to 20° C. (65 to 68° F.) and the application of only as much water as is needed to keep the leaves from drooping. Feed should be applied weekly until the plant flowers and then again after an interval of a month. Aphelandra is a very handsome and decorative house plant which requires liberal watering except during the winter months. The foliage is very ornamental and young plants are an attractive decoration in the window glasshouse or plant case.

Aphelandra squarrosa NEES var. *louisae*

Ardisia SW.
Coral Berry

This is a lovely house plant of shrub-like habit with persistent, simple, leathery leaves and small white to pinkish flowers. The fruit is a berry. The genus *Ardisia* comprises some 400 species native to the tropics and subtropics.

Most commonly grown is *Ardisia crispa* from China. Propagation is from the seed or by cuttings. The seeds, sown in pans of sand, require a temperature of 20 to 22° C. (68 to 72° F.). When four or five leaflets have been formed then seedlings should be moved into small pots with a mixture of equal parts of leafmould, peat and sand. The following spring the plants should be transferred to 4-in. (10-cm.) pots in John Innes or a peat-based compost. Immediately after repotting the plants should be watered sparingly, or, better still, only sprayed over. For cultivation indoors it is possible to purchase plants that already have berries.

During the summer months the plants should be placed by a closed window, shielded from the mid-day sun and drafts, and watered liberally with an occasional application of liquid feed so that the leaves will turn dark and the berries develop well. From winter until spring it is not only the foliage but also the scarlet berries which make the plant such an attractive ornament. During the winter months keep the plant in a light place at a temperature of 15° C. (59° F.) and water moderately. It should be repotted every spring in March. Coral berry was at one time widely cultivated as a house plant and even today it is often seen in flower shops where it stands out amidst the other plants.

Ardisia crispa A. DC.

Asparagus L.
Asparagus Fern

Of the 150 species native to the Mediterranean region and Africa the best known is *Asparagus densiflorus* 'Sprengeri', (syn. *A. sprengeri*) from West Africa. It is a semi-shrub of greatly branching habit with stems of quadrangular section bearing phylloclades, which are leaf-like branches that have taken over the function of leaves. The true leaves in this instance are the long sharp spines. Another commonly grown species is *A. setaceus* (syn. *A. plumosus*) from Cape Town with very slender stems and long fine phylloclades. Both are grown as pot plants as well as for cutting.

In nurseries they are propagated from the seed, in the home mainly by division in spring. In the case of *A. densiflorus* care should be taken during transplanting and division not to damage the white thickened storage organs on the roots. The divided sections should be put in moderately large pots in John Innes or a peat-based compost. *A. densiflorus* should be placed in the lightest position in the room. In summer it benefits by being put out on the balcony or in the garden, being moved back to a pot and placed indoors again in September. Asparagus requires liberal watering and an occasional application of liquid feed. Young plants should be repotted every year in March, older plants at longer intervals. *A. setaceus* should be grown indoors throughout the year as it requires slight shade. In winter a temperature of 10 to 15° C. (50 to 59° F.) is sufficient for both species.

Asparagus setaceus JESSOP

Asplenium L.

Spleenwort

Spleenworts are ferns with short stems and persistent fronds of greatly diverse forms and linear sori (capsules borne on the underside of the fronds which contain the spores). There are 200 known species of the genus distributed throughout the world.

Asplenium nidus is an epiphytic fern from tropical Asia and Australia with pale green, parchment-like leaves forming a funnel-shaped rosette. It grows well as a pot plant and its leaves make it a striking ornament. Young plants should be repotted every year, older ones every two or three years. They should be put in a mixture of two parts leafmould, two parts peat and one part sand (or in a peat-based compost or John Innes with added peat) and placed in a spot with good light, but not right by a window. In winter they should be kept at a temperature of 12 to 18° C. (54 to 65° F.). They require a moist atmosphere. Young plants are a lovely decorative element in a window glasshouse or indoor glass case.

Asplenium bulbiferum from Australia has leaves up to 20 in. (50 cm.) long and 8 to 12 in. (20 to 30 cm.) across, with margins on which buds with roots (bulbils) form. This lovely fern is particularly well suited to cold rooms. It is easily propagated by means of the young plants which grow on the margins of the leaves. These are separated from the leaf and planted close together in a dish, from which they should be moved to small individual pots. In winter this spleenwort requires a temperature of 8 to 10° C. (46 to 50° F.).

Asplenium nidus L.

Begonia L.

Begonias are mostly herbaceous plants with succulent, fleshy stems and variously shaped, variegated leaves. There are terrestrial as well as epiphytic forms. Approximately 1,000 species are native to the tropical regions of Asia, Africa and America. The species and hybrids are divided into three groups: tuberous, leafy and shrubby forms.

Begonias are generally propagated by vegetative means. Tall shrub begonias are propagated by stem cuttings taken from the tip, species that do not form stems by leaf cuttings. These may be taken at any time of the year but spring is the best when old plants are being repotted. Cuttings should be put into clean pots in a mixture of peat and sand. Stem cuttings from the tip should be trimmed to a length of 3 in. (8 cm.), leaf cuttings of whole leaves should be taken with a 1-in. (2.5-cm.) length of stalk. It is also possible to cut whole leaves into sections and make cuttings of these. The pot with the cuttings should be covered with a glass jar or plastic bag and placed by a window, the required temperature being 20° C. (68° F.). When the cuttings have rooted they should be potted up into 3-in. (8-cm.) pots in a mixture of four parts peat, two parts leafmould and one part sand (or John Innes or a peat-based compost). Later in the summer they should be potted on into larger pots. In summer begonias should be kept a short distance from the window in partial shade and watered when necessary, with an occasional application of feed. In winter the plants should be watered less frequently and placed in a light spot with a temperature of 15 to 18° C. (59 to 65° F.). Although some species are rather exacting when it comes to cultivation, others do just as well indoors as other house plants.

Begonia × 'Corallina de Lucerna'

Bertolonia RADDI

There are about six known species of bertolonias, perennial herbaceous plants of low habit with large, ovate, entire, variegated leaves,
native to southern Brazil. Most commonly grown are *Bertolonia
marmorata* and *B. maculata,* which are propagated by seed or by
cuttings. Seeds are sown in March in a pan filled with clean, rough
peat. They should be sown thinly on the surface, which has been
previously levelled. The dish should then be covered with a glass jar
or plastic bag and kept at a temperature of 22° C. (72° F.). Two
weeks after germination the seedlings should be pricked out into
a pot in a mixture of two parts peat, one part leafmould, one part
cut sphagnum and one part sand and kept covered with a glass jar
or plastic bag. When they are strong enough they should be potted
up in threes into 4-in. (10-cm.) pots and put in a window glasshouse
or plant case. Cuttings should be inserted in a mixture of one part
peat and one part sand in a propagator with bottom heat. They
will root within three weeks, after which they should be transferred
into the same mixture as the seedlings.

With their habit of growth and richly coloured leaves bertolonias
are among the loveliest of tropical plants. Indoors they should be
kept in a moderately shaded position and provided with sufficient
warmth and a moist atmosphere. The leaves should not be watered
as this is detrimental to the plants. They are attractive in window
glasshouses or plant cases where they do very well. Bertolonias do
not have a winter rest period and should, therefore, be watered
and kept at a temperature of at least 20° C. (68° F.) even during the
winter months. The illustrated species, *Bertonerila houtteana* hort.,
is the result of inter-generic breeding between the genera *Bertolonia*
and *Sonerila.*

Bertonerila houtteana hort.

Billbergia THUNB.
Queen's Tears

Bromeliaceae

The 50 to 60 known species of this genus are natives of southern Mexico, Bolivia and northern Argentina. They are mostly epiphytic plants with stiff leaves arranged in a rosette and sprays of flowers, often pendent, with reddish bracts. One of the best known species is *Billbergia nutans,* which forms a rosette of ten to fifteen leathery leaves that are 12 in. (30 cm.) long and $\frac{1}{2}$ in. (1 cm.) across. The flowers are yellow, edged with deep blue and subtended by pale pink bracts. *B. windii* has bright pink bracts and violet-blue flowers.

Billbergias are transplanted in spring or summer, after the flowers have faded, into a mixture of two parts leafmould, two parts peat and one part sand or a peat-based compost or John Innes with additional peat. When moving the plants they may be increased by division of the clumps. At first they should be placed by a closed window because they require a great deal of light. From January until July they should be given a light application of liquid feed once a week. Billbergias are very good plants for rooms with central heating as the dry atmosphere promotes richer coloration of the bracts; 15 to 25° C. (59 to 77° F.) is the most favourable temperature during the growing period while 15 to 18° C. (59 to 65° F.) will suffice in winter, but then it is necessary to keep the compost dryer. This will increase the plants' hardiness and will make it easier for them to survive the critical winter period. In general, it may be said that billbergias are of very easy culture and are among the hardiest of all house plants.

Billbergia saundersii hort. BULL ex DOMBR.

Bougainvillea COMM ex JUSS.
mut. CHOISY.

Nyctaginaceae

These are climbing shrubs, partly thorny, with alternate simple leaves. The insignificant flowers are borne at the ends of short side branches and are subtended by heart-shaped bracts coloured pink, violet or red according to the given species. There are eight species of this genus, all native to South America.

Propagation is by means of cuttings from young shoots, about 2½ in. (6 cm.) long, which are inserted in a pot of sand, covered with a glass jar or plastic bag and put by a closed window. Cuttings root best indoors if they are taken in June. When they have produced roots, which is within three weeks, they should be potted up into 3-in. (8-cm.) pots; it is important to handle them very carefully as the roots are extremely fragile. The mixture in which they are planted should consist of two parts leafmould, one part loam and one part sand or John Innes or a peat-based compost. At first the cuttings should be placed by a closed window but as soon as they take root the window should be opened. At the end of July pot them on to larger, 4-in. (10-cm.) pots. In winter the young plants should be kept by a window at a temperature of 10 to 12° C. (50 to 54° F.) and watered only slightly.

In the second year the plants may be put out of doors in summer or by an open window in full sunlight. Stronger plants require a period of rest during the winter, at which time they should be kept rather dry and at a low temperature. Watering may be resumed in late February with liquid feed being applied at regular intervals. The plants will begin to bloom at the end of March. When they have finished flowering they should be repotted and pruned partly back.

Bougainvillea × *buttiana* HOLTT. et STANDL. 'Mrs Butt'

Caladium VENT.

These are tuberous-rooted perennials comprising some 16 species native to tropical America. They are grown for their richly coloured, ornamental leaves which are heart shaped and have long stalks. The head of flowers is concealed by a spathe.

The species *Caladium bicolor* is the one generally cultivated. This has dark green leaves with white or reddish spots or veins. The growing season is comparatively short and during the dormant period the leaves die off. In winter the tubers should be kept dry in their pots at a temperature of 16 to 18° C. (60 to 65° F.). In March they should be tipped out and cleaned and then repotted into 5-in. (13-cm.) pots in a mixture of four parts leafmould, two parts peat and one part sand (or John Innes potting compost with extra peat). The young plants should be put in a warm spot with plenty of light. Light is a very important requirement, for otherwise the leaves tend to grow too long. Caladiums need warmth and a moist atmosphere during the growing period and for this reason do best in a window glasshouse or by a closed window. They should be watered liberally throughout the summer. In October, when the leaves begin to turn yellow, watering should be gradually decreased until it is stopped altogether. The dried-off tubers should be put in a dark, dry and warm place in their pots and started again in the spring of the following year. Even though caladiums are not as beautiful nor as large when grown in a room instead of in a greenhouse, they are still very ornamental.

Caladium bicolor VENT.

Calathea G. F. W. MEY.   *Marantaceae*

These are attractive perennial foliage plants. The leaves, borne on long stalks, are asymmetrical with a marked mid-rib. Calatheas are very similar to marantas and are often mistaken for them; however, calatheas are of taller and more upright habit whereas marantas are spreading plants. The 100 or so species of *Calathea* are native to tropical America.

Most often grown as a house plant is *Calathea makoyana* (syn. *Maranta makoyana* hort.), which reaches a height of 12 in. (30 cm.) and has broadly oblong leaves with dark green blotches. *C. ornata* (syn. *Maranta ornata*) has elliptical leaves, striped pink when young. *C. insignis* has oblong, pointed leaves with black-green markings.

Cultivation is the same for both calathea and maranta. The plants may be propagated by division when they are being repotted in February or March. Some species form young plants on the flower stalks, which when separated and kept in sand at a temperature of 20 to 22° C. (68 to 72° F.) will take root rapidly. Rooted cuttings are then potted up, two or three to a pot, in a mixture of one part each of leafmould, peat, loam and sand. John Innes or a peat-based compost may also be used. In summer they should be given liquid feed in weak solution. If grown as house plants both calatheas and marantas are best kept in window glasshouses or in indoor glass cases where they can be provided throughout the year with the conditions they require, namely a temperature of 20 to 22° C. (68 to 72° F.) and sufficient atmospheric moisture.

Calathea insignis BOOM.

Camellia L.   *Theaceae*

Camellias are shrubs or trees with dark green, glossy, leathery leaves which are simple and persistent. The sessile flowers are borne singly or in clusters of two or three. There are more than 80 species of *Camellia* native to India, Japan and China.

Camellia japonica is the best known and is grown in a wide variety of forms. It flowers from November until April. Propagation by cuttings is difficult but the procedure is as follows: cuttings, 2½ to 3 in. (6 to 8 cm.) long, should be taken from the tips of the stems in February, March or August and put into a mixture of equal parts of peat and sand in a propagator with bottom heat which keeps the rooting medium at a temperature of 25° C. (77° F.). After they have rooted the cuttings are potted up into small pots in a mixture of two parts peat and one part each of leafmould and sand. Young plants should be repotted every spring after flowering, older specimens every two to four years.

During the summer camellias can be placed by an open window with a northern exposure or in a shady spot in the garden. They should be watered with soft or rain water and fed every second week. The plants are intolerant of both overwatering and over-dry conditions. In winter keep them by a window in a cool room which has plenty of light at a temperature of 4 to 10° C. (39 to 50° F.). Plants with buds must not be turned nor moved frequently from one spot to another. The leaves should be sponged regularly. On bright days the plants benefit by being sprayed with water in the morning. As soon as the buds start to colour, however, spraying should be stopped, but water should be applied to the soil more liberally.

Camellia japonica L. 'Chandleri Elegans'

Cattleya LINDL.   *Orchidaceae*
Cattleya Orchid

These are epiphytic orchids with large rootstocks and stems swollen
into egg-shaped or cylindrical tubers from each of which arise one
or two thick, leathery leaves. The flowers are borne singly or in
clusters and measure 2½ to 10 in. (6 to 25 cm.) across. This genus
contains 40 species native to tropical America. The dormant period
of many species grown in Europe occurs in the autumn and winter
months, during which time watering should be considerably limited,
the supply being increased again as soon as the buds appear. Autumn-
and winter-flowering species should be repotted in March when they
begin to put out new roots. Species that flower in June should be
repotted after the flowers have faded.

Cattleya orchids should be planted in a mixture for epiphytic
orchids (page 14) and should be watered once after they have been
repotted but then kept dry until they put out new roots. At the same
time, or shortly after the roots appear, a new shoot begins to sprout
from the bud of the last tuber and water should be applied more
liberally; fresh air and shade are also necessary. As soon as the tuber
has reached its full growth watering must be considerably limited.
At this time the plants must be given more light and air to ensure
the ripening of the tuber. When a new bud appears watering is
resumed and continued until flowering has finished. The plant
should be shielded from the hot mid-day sun. In winter cattleya
orchids need to be kept at a temperature of 14° C. (58° F.) during
the daytime and 12° C. (54° F.) at night, in summer 22° C. (72° F.)
during the daytime and 18° C. (65° F.) at night.

Cattleya labiata LINDL.

Chamaedorea WILLD.   *Palmae*

Chamaedoreas are small, low palms of shrub-like habit with slender stems and simple leaves which sometimes have toothed margins. The 60 species that make up the genus are all natives of Central America.

Most commonly grown as a pot plant is *C. elegans* from Mexico, older specimens of which bear orange-red flowers. Young palms should be repotted after one year, older specimens after three to five years. Chamaedoreas are propagated either by seed or by suckers. Seeds should be sown in sand in pots and put in a warm and moist environment. Seedlings should be pricked out into pots either singly or in twos and when they have rooted well should be potted on into larger pots in John Innes potting compost. It is recommended to use full sized rather than shallow pots. During the growing period chamaedoreas should be supplied with warmth, moisture and moderate shade and given an occasional application of liquid feed. In winter they should be kept at a temperature of about 15° C. (59° F.). The soil should be watered moderately but frequent spraying with tepid water is recommended. The plants also benefit from an occasional sponging of the leaves. If the leaves are attacked by aphids they should be sprayed with a protective agent.

These elegant palms are most effective indoors if potted singly, as solitary specimens. Chamaedoreas are among the best palms for pot cultivation being ideally suited to flats with little space. However, it must be borne in mind that they are sensitive to changes in temperature.

Chamaedorea elegans MART.

Cissus L.   *Vitaceae*
Kangaroo Vine

These are either woody, vine-like climbers with clinging tendrils or shrubs. Some species are succulents, others large herbaceous plants. In all, there are more than 300 known species native to the tropics.

Most commonly grown as a house plant is *Cissus antarctica*. Propagation is solely by cuttings which may be taken at any time of the year but are best in spring or summer. The cutting taken from the tip of the stem should be trimmed to a length of 4 in. (10 cm.) and the remainder of the shoot cut into pieces with two to three leaves to each section. Put the cuttings into a propagator in a mixture of two parts peat and one part sand and cover with a glass jar or sheet of glass. At a temperature of 20° C. (68° F.) they will root within three weeks, after which they should be potted up into 3-in. (8-cm.) pots in a mixture of two parts leafmould, two parts loam and one each of peat and sand or John Innes or a peat-based compost. Put the potted cuttings by a closed window in a temperature of 18 to 20° C. (65 to 68° F.). Water the plants sparingly at first, then more freely as the cuttings become established. Smaller plants should be repotted every spring, older plants after two or three years.

In recent years many species of *Cissus* have been cultivated as ornamental house plants, grown in hanging baskets, as shaped and contoured solitary specimens, or several smaller plants in one container. They have no particular preference with regard to location. In a warm spot they need to be watered more liberally, in a cool one they should be watered less. Occasional applications of liquid feed are beneficial to growth. *C. antarctica* may be put out of doors in summer.

Cissus antarctica VENT.

Citrus L.

The members of this genus, numbering some 12 species from eastern Asia, are citrus shrubs or trees, often covered with spines. The leaves are alternate, leathery and may be persistent or deciduous. The flowers are borne in cymes and have a lovely fragrance. *Fortunella japonica (Citrus japonica)* is one of the kinds often grown as a pot plant.

Citrus plants are propagated by means of cuttings inserted in sand in a propagator with bottom heat, or by grafting when the sap is flowing. Cuttings, buds or grafts are taken from fruit-bearing shrubs. Younger plants should be repotted every spring before they begin active growth, older ones after an interval of several years. The potting mixture should consist of equal parts of loam, peat and sand, or John Innes potting compost can be used. After repotting, the plants should be put by a closed window and watered with care. When they have become established and during the summer months they should be placed by an open window, or, better still, on a balcony or out in the garden with the pot plunged into the soil. In summer water should be applied liberally and the plants should be given an occasional application of liquid feed. In spring, when they are in bloom, it is recommended to transfer pollen from one flower to another with a brush in order to have a greater quantity of fruits. Citrus plants are not fond of artificial heat and in winter do best in a light, unheated room to which the door from another, heated room may be opened on occasion to let some warmth in. A temperature of 12 to 14° C. (54 to 58° F.) is sufficient during the winter months and this may be even lower if water is applied sparingly. The fruits (only those which follow the spring flowering are allowed to remain on the plant) are quite large but, depending on the species grown, may be inedible.

Fortunella japonica SWINGLE

Clivia LINDL.

There are three species of *Clivia*, all native to South Africa. The leaves, arranged in two rows, are stiff, strap-like, 1 to 2½ in. (2.5 to 6 cm.) wide and up to 20 in. (50 cm.) long. The roots are thick and fleshy. The stem is topped by a cluster of ten to twenty blooms.

Most commonly grown is *Clivia miniata*, which sometimes bears more than twenty bright orange-red flowers. Young plantlets are separated from the parent plant during the spring repotting after the flowers have faded. To obtain plants that will flower as soon as possible after division let the plantlets grow on the parent plant for as long as two years before separating them. Older plants should be repotted every few years into a mixture of equal parts of leafmould, peat, loam and sand or John Innes or a peat-based compost. The size of the pots chosen for repotting both older and younger plants depends on the abundance of roots. It is always better to use a smaller pot than one that is too large. After repotting water should be applied moderately. Clivias like a semi-shaded position. Established plants should be watered liberally in summer, but at the end of September watering should be cut back sharply. During the winter the plants should be kept at a temperature of 8 to 10° C. (46 to 50° F.) though they are tolerant of higher temperatures. When buds appear water should again be applied more liberally. After the flowers have faded the stem should be cut back so there is no loss of strength due to seed formation.

Clivia miniata REGEL.

94

Cocos L. *Palmae*

These palms with their slender, ringed stems (the rings are leaf scars) and rich, symmetrical fronds make lovely house plants. The 50 or so species, some of them short-stemmed, are all native to tropical America.

Most commonly cultivated in the home is *Cocos weddelliana* (syn. *Syagrus weddelliana, Microcoelum weddelianum*) — a slow-growing palm of delicate appearance that may be used as an ornament even in smaller rooms with north-facing windows. In winter it requires a temperature of 18 to 20° C. (65 to 68° F.). The root ball must never be allowed to dry out and it does not matter if some water remains in the bottom of the container after watering. The plant benefits greatly from frequent overhead spraying, especially in homes with central heating. From February until September it should be given a weekly application of liquid feed. This palm is usually offered for sale in small pots and, therefore, should be potted on in spring into a larger pot in a mixture of two parts leafmould, two parts peat, two parts loam and one part sand, or John Innes potting compost. Further repotting should be carried out at intervals of several years. Spraying with insecticides protects the plant against pests. Even though this palm is not long lived as a pot plant, it is very popular with many growers. It may be used as a solitary specimen or in a group with other plants needing similar treatment.

Cocos weddelliana H. WENDL. (syn. *Syagrus weddelliana* BECC.)

Codiaeum A. JUSS.

Croton

Crotons are shrubby plants with alternate, entire, evergreen leaves. There are about 16 species, all native to Indonesia and the islands of the Pacific.

Most commonly grown is *Codiaeum variegatum,* which is propagated by vegetative means. A good method is by air-layering — making a cut in the stem and wrapping it first in damp moss and then in plastic. After a month, when well-developed roots appear, cut off the top and pot it up. Another good method of propagation is by means of cuttings. Only ripe tip cuttings, 4 in. (10 cm.) long, should be taken, and these should be inserted in a mixture of three parts peat and one part sand in a propagator supplied with bottom heat to at least 25° C. (77° F.). When they have rooted, which takes about a month, they can be potted into 3-in. (8-cm.) pots and kept in a warm and moist spot. Later, after they have become well established, they will need repotting into larger pots. The potting mixture should consist of two parts leafmould, one part peat and one part sand, or John Innes or a peat-based compost.

Crotons are grown indoors throughout the year. Young plants do best in a window glasshouse or indoor glass case where there is sufficient warmth and atmospheric moisture. Older plants may be placed by a closed window with a southern exposure. Repot plants in spring. In summer water liberally and spray the leaves, also apply feed more frequently. In winter crotons will survive only if kept indoors in a spot where the temperature does not fall below 15° C. (59° F.).

Codiaeum variegatum A. JUSS. var. *pictum* MÜLL. ARG.

Coelogyne LINDL.   *Orchidaceae*

Coelogynes are epiphytic or terrestrial orchids with prostrate stems and bulbs from which arise one or two evergreen leaves. The flowers, with practically identical pendulous petals, are borne in clusters. There are about 150 known species that grow wild in the monsoon zone.

Most commonly grown as a house plant is *Coelogyne cristata* from the Himalayas. The bulb has two lanceolate leaves measuring 10 in. (25 cm.) in length and 1 in. (2.5 cm.) across. The flower clusters each consist of five to nine blossoms. These are snow white with five yellow ribs and are borne from January till March. Propagation is by division when the orchids are being repotted, the best time being March when the plants put out new roots. The potting mixture is the one used for epiphytic orchids (page 14) and large, shallow dishes are the best containers as the plants spread outwards. Annual repotting is not recommended; all that needs to be done is to remove old, dead bulbs and fill the gaps with a new soil mixture. Plants that are not repotted should be given a weekly application of liquid manure. During the growing season coelogynes require warm, fresh air and light shade. By the end of August the new bulbs are already well developed and should be given less water and more fresh air and light. In winter keep the plants drier at a temperature of 10 to 12° C. (50 to 54° F.). Only after the flower buds develop should watering be increased. Coelogyne should be placed by a window where it has plenty of light.

Coelogyne cristata LINDL.

Coleus LOUR.

Labiatae

These are tropical species of herbaceous plants or semi-shrubs, usually with variegated foliage and small flowers. The 150 species are natives of Africa and Asia. The only ones cultivated by growers are the varieties of *Coleus blumei,* which have 12- to 16-in. (30- to 40-cm.) angular stems and pointed egg-shaped leaves with coarsely serrated margins and variegated colouring. Many forms, previously listed under various names, were developed from this species.

Propagation is by seeds or by cuttings. Sow the seeds in spring into pots, where they will germinate rapidly at a temperature of 18° C. (65° F.). The seedlings should be pricked out into a light, sandy soil and later potted up into small and then larger pots. Some forms do not bear flowers and must, therefore, be perpetuated by cuttings. These should be taken in spring and put in a glass with water or in a pot of sand and covered with a glass jar until roots are formed. The rooted cuttings can be potted up and placed by a closed window. Later, in June, they should be potted on into larger pots using a mixture of two parts peat, four parts loam and one part sand, or John Innes potting compost. During the summer months the plants can stand in direct sunlight on the windowsill. They need liberal watering and a weekly feed. In winter coleus requires a temperature of 16 to 18° C. (60 to 65° F.), light, and drier conditions. Plants should be repotted only in March. Coleus is available in various colours and is of very easy culture.

Coleus blumei-Hybrid

Cordyline COMM. EX JUSS.

Agavaceae

These are small, palm-like plants with sword-shaped leaves forming a crown on a slender trunk, which is usually bulbous at the base. About 20 species, resembling dracaenas, are natives of Asia, Africa and Australia. One of the loveliest is *Cordyline terminalis* from which numerous hybrids coloured wine red, red and white, yellow and green, etc. have been developed.

Cordyline terminalis should be propagated in early spring by means of tip cuttings taken from plants that have no leaves at the base of the stem. The cuttings should be inserted in small pots in a mixture of peat and sand with added cut sphagnum and placed in a propagator with a minimum temperature of 22 to 25° C. (72 to 77° F.). They will be well rooted within three weeks. On removal of the tip all that is left of the plant is a bare stem which can be cut up into 2-in. (5-cm.)-long sections; if these are then put bottom end downwards in a propagator they will also grow into fine specimens. Rooted cuttings should be put first in 3-in. (8-cm.) pots and in summer potted on into larger, 5-in. (13-cm.) pots in a mixture of four parts leafmould, two parts peat and one part sand, or John Innes potting compost may be used. The following year they will need to be potted on into still larger pots. In summer the plants should be shielded from direct sunlight and given a weekly application of feed; in winter they require a well-lit situation. Older plants are repotted in spring every two or three years. For good growth they require a temperature of 20 to 25° C. (68 to 77°.F.) in summer; the lowest permissible winter temperature is 15° C. (59° F.) and then only for a short period.

Cordyline terminalis KUNTH 'Tricolor'

Cryptanthus OTTO & DIETR.   *Bromeliaceae*

These small terrestrial bromeliads sometimes also grow as epiphytes. The 20 or so species originate from eastern Brazil where they cover whole areas of open forests. They form star-shaped rosettes at ground level (hence their common name terrestrial stars) of finely toothed leaves that are usually variegated. The small white flowers are borne in the centre of each rosette. Propagation is usually by means of the shoots that grow from the centre of the rosette after the flowers have faded. These should be put in small pots (several to one container) in a mixture recommended for epiphytic bromeliads (page 15).

Cryptanthus should be kept in a warm and well-lit situation throughout the year, even in winter the temperature should not drop below 16° C. (60° F.). The plants are intolerant of direct sunlight. As the plants do not require a resting period the soil should be kept sufficiently moist both in summer and winter. Care should be taken not to wet the leaves when watering as this will damage the ornamental waxy scales. In summer the plants appreciate an occasional application of a weak solution of liquid feed.

Cryptanthus is gaining in popularity with amateur growers. It is suitable for planting on branches as well as in bowls and does particularly well in window glasshouses, indoor glass cases and terrariums where there is sufficient warmth and atmospheric moisture. It also grows well in rooms.

Cryptanthus bivittatus REGEL.

Cyclamen L.

Primulaceae

Cyclamens are low perennial herbaceous plants with underground tuberous roots. The leaves, borne on long stalks, are heart shaped and patterned with light veins. The flowers have ovate recurved petals which are curled up tightly in the bud. There are 20 species, all native to southern Europe and the Mediterranean region. The only one grown as a house plant is *Cyclamen persicum giganteum* from Asia Minor.

If good plants with plenty of buds are purchased in September and given proper care they will flower until April. The plants should be placed on the windowsill and watered from below but, as plants should not stand in water, any that is not absorbed by the soil after an hour should be poured off. Since cyclamens flower chiefly in winter they may also be given a weak solution of liquid feed at this time; this should be put only in the dish in which the pots stand. In the case of severe frosts the plants should be moved away from the window and stood in a light place inside the room. After flowering in May the plants can be moved out of doors to a shady spot on the balcony or in the garden and watered only lightly. In early September clean the plants and put them back in the window. They should not be repotted, only given an application of liquid feed every now and then. In winter they do best at a temperature of 8 to 12° C. (46 to 54° F.).

Cyclamen persicum MILL. *giganteum*

Cymbidium sw.

Orchidaceae

Cymbidiums are either epiphytic or terrestrial orchids with short stems swollen at the base into flattened bulbs with numerous linear leaves. The flower stems may be as much as 3 ft. (1 m.) long with fifteen to twenty dainty blooms that are very long lived. There are some 50 species of *Cymbidium,* native to the tropic and subtropic regions of Madagascar, Asia and Australia.

Young plants should be potted on every year after flowering, older plants after several years, into a mixture for terrestrial orchids (page 14). After repotting apply water sparingly for a period of six weeks. At the end of May harden the plants off and later move them out of doors. In summer they do best in semi-shade by an open window, on a balcony or in the garden in the shade of a tree. They must not be allowed to become dry during the growing period. Apply water liberally and give a weak solution of liquid feed. They will grow better if they are plunged with their pots into peat or moss. In late August when the bulbs have ripened, gradually decrease the application of water until it is withheld almost entirely. In autumn and winter cymbidiums should be kept in a cool, dry and light spot at a temperature of 8 to 10° C. (46 to 50° F.). As warmth and light increase with the lengthening days of spring buds begin to form and at this time watering should be resumed. More robust specimens may have several sprays of flowers.

Cymbidium-Hybrid

Cyperus L.

These are perennial plants with stems terminated by rosettes of spreading leaves from the centres of which arise spike-shaped inflorescences. Some 400 species are to be found in regions with a warm and mild climate.

Most commonly grown as a house plant is *Cyperus alternifolius* from Madagascar. The 1½- to 3-ft. (45- to 90-cm.)-long stem ends in a tuft of horizontally spreading leaves. *C. natalensis* is 10 to 12 in (25 to 30 cm.) tall and forms compact clumps. The leaves are dark green and measure ½ in. (1 cm.) across. Leaf cuttings from *C. alternifolius* taken with a ¾-in. (2-cm.) stalk will soon take root when inserted about three-quarters of an inch (2 cm.) into a glass filled with water. To obtain stronger specimens pot up rooted cuttings in small pots, two to three to a pot, moving them later to larger pots. Stronger, older plants, particularly specimens of *C. natalensis,* may be increased also by division of clumps when repotting in spring. The potting mixture should consist of equal parts of leafmould, peat, loam and sand, or John Innes potting compost may be used.

Cyperus should be kept in a well-lit spot, best of all by a window, and given liquid feed from spring until autumn. In winter it requires a temperature of 12 to 18° C. (54 to 65° F.). Cyperus are bog plants and, therefore, when cultivated in rooms the pots must be stood in a dish of water so that the roots are kept moist. Cyperus is useful as a companion plant for the aquarium.

Cyperus alternifolius L.

Dendrobium sw.   *Orchidaceae*

Dendrobiums are epiphytic orchids with long segmented stems and either deciduous or persistent leaves. The 900 or so species are to be found in the tropics and subtropics. The most widespread is *Dendrobium nobile* and its hybrids. This bears flowers on two-year-old bulbs after the leaves have been shed.

Dendrobiums require warmth, moisture and light during the growing period and a dry, cooler environment during the rest period. Only warmth-loving species, such as *D. phalaenopsis*, are kept in a warmer environment throughout, even in winter. The growing period is usually from March until August but some warmth-loving species do not begin growing until May. Dendrobiums should be repotted shortly before they begin making new roots into a mixture recommended for epiphytic orchids (page 14), but not every year. They should be kept in a sunny spot and during the summer months the plants should be watered as well as sprayed with water and supplied with plenty of fresh air.

In the case of deciduous species water should be withheld from late September. On two-year-old bulbs the leaves turn yellow and fall, after which the bulbs should be kept in a dry and light situation at a temperature of 8 to 10° C. (46 to 50° F.) for a period of about three months. After this, when buds begin to form, the temperature should be raised and watering resumed; the plants will then flower within six weeks. It is imperative that the plants are given the required period of rest, otherwise they grow but do not flower. Such are the conditions in their native environment. Dendrobiums serve as good examples of how important it is to provide plants with the same conditions in the home as they have in nature.

Dendrobiums grown as pot plants may be increased by division of clumps when repotting and by means of the small plantlets that grow out from the bulbs.

Dendrobium nobile LINDL. var. *sanderianum* hort.

Dracaena VAND. EX L.   *Agavaceae*
Corn Plant

Dracaenas are woody plants with simple or forked trunks and narrow, lanceolate to sword-shaped leaves arranged in dense spirals. The 10 or so species are native to the tropical and subtropical regions of Asia and Africa, and are closely related to the genus *Cordyline*.

Mostly grown in the home are the brightly variegated foliage plants such as *Dracaena deremensis* and *D. fragrans*, which require semi-shade. A good time to propagate dracaenas is in spring or summer and air-layering has proved to be the best method. This consists of making a deep longitudinal cut into the semi-woody stem at the top, wrapping the cut in moss (best of all sphagnum), and enclosing this in a plastic sheet tied at the top and bottom. The plant is then placed by a closed window where it will make roots within four to five weeks. As soon as the roots are visible cut off the top part of the stem and put it, together with the moss packing, into a sufficiently large pot in a mixture of four parts leafmould, two parts peat and one part sand. Later in summer it should be potted on into a larger pot in the mixture just described or John Innes or a peat-based compost. If the plants are well established in summer they should be watered liberally and given an application of liquid feed now and then. In winter a good temperature is between 15 and 18° C. (59 to 65° F.) but they must be watered continually, albeit lightly. Dracaenas should be repotted every two or three years in April. In the home they are generally grown as solitary specimens.

Dracaena deremensis ENGL. cv. 'Bausei'

116

Drosera L.
Sundew or Youth-wort

The genus *Drosera* comprises some 85 species native to Brazil, Central America, tropical Africa and Europe. These plants have numerous glands on the upper leaf surfaces which secrete a viscous fluid that glitters in the sun and attracts small insects. Two species can be grown as house plants: *Drosera capensis* and *D. spathulata*.

Droseras are generally propagated from seeds and do best in shallow pans about 4 in. (10 cm.) high. Sow the seeds thinly in March in rough moist peat mixed with a little sand. Do not cover the seeds with soil for they need plenty of light, but until germination occurs keep them covered with a glass jar or plastic bag. The pan with the seeds should be placed in a larger dish of water so that the substrate is continually moist. At a temperature of 16 to 18° C. (60 to 65° F.) the seeds will germinate within three weeks. Droseras require lots of light and air and the seedlings should be put in the window in full sunlight and aired now and then. Two months after germination the seedlings can be pricked out in threes spaced 1 in. (2.5 cm.) apart in pots of fresh compost consisting of the same mixture as the sowing medium. Use a small wooden fork or plant label for this purpose. The pot containing the pricked-out seedlings should again be placed in a dish of water. During the winter both species are kept by the window at a temperature of 8 to 10° C. (46 to 50° F.). They flower in spring.

Drosera spathulata LABILL.

Euphorbia L.
Spurge

Euphorbias are herbaceous plants or semi-shrubs of widely varied form. The leaves are simple, alternate or in rosettes, heart shaped or oblong. There are also leafless species with spherical or pear-shaped bodies. All have a milky sap which is often poisonous. There are about 1600 species of spurge distributed throughout the world except in the arctic zone.

Most commonly grown as a house plant is *Euphorbia milii* (syn. *E. splendens*), crown of thorns, from Madagascar. It seldom needs repotting, but in order to encourage branching the tips should be cut off in June, care being taken that the poisonous milky sap does not get into the eyes or an open wound. The removed tips can be used as cuttings — trim them to lengths of 2½ to 3 in. (6 to 8 cm.), dip the cut ends in powdered charcoal and leave them exposed to the air for two days. Then clean the cut surfaces and insert the cuttings in pots in a mixture of clean coarse sand and bits of charcoal. Because cuttings are taken in summer no bottom heat is required but the pot should be put in a shady place. Moisten the sand thoroughly before inserting the cuttings, afterwards water should be supplied whenever the sand dries out. When they have rooted, the cuttings should be potted up into small pots in John Innes potting compost with extra sand, and watered as required to keep the root ball from drying out. Feed should be given at two-week intervals. Place the plants in a spot with plenty of light. In winter spurge should be kept in a light situation at a temperature of 10 to 12° C. (50 to 54° F.).

Euphorbia milii DESMOULINS

x *Fatshedera* GUILLAUMIN.

Araliaceae

× Fatshedera is a hybrid between *Fatsia japonica* and *Hedera helix,* bred by Frères Lize in Nantes in 1910, and like both parents it is also an evergreen plant. It is a shrub with slender trunk, upright at first and later prostrate. Propagation is solely by cuttings, which may be taken at any time of the year but preferably in spring before new growth begins. The tip cutting, with three to four leaves, and the stem sections, each with one leaf, should be inserted in a pot of sand. At a temperature of 18 to 20° C. (65 to 68° F.) they will root rapidly, after which they should be potted up into 3-in. (8-cm.) pots in sandy loam and in summer potted on again into 5-in. (13-cm.) pots. During the summer months place the plants by an open window with a northern exposure or in a shaded spot in the garden. During the growing period the plants should be watered liberally and occasionally given an application of a weak solution of liquid feed.

× Fatshedera has no particular requirements and is a very good plant for cold rooms and corridors provided the temperature does not drop below freezing point. It is a shade-loving plant and should be repotted every spring before the new growth begins. Older plants should be staked.

× *Fatshedera lizei* GUILLAUMIN.

Ficus L.
Rubber Plant

The genus *Ficus* includes woody plants of widely varied forms — epiphytic slender-branched climbers as well as shrubs and trees of upright habit. The 2,000 or so species of this genus are native to the tropics and subtropics, and the most widely distributed of the lot is *Ficus elastica*.

All species of *Ficus* are propagated by air-layering and June, when it is warmer, is the best time. At the spot where you wish the plant top to make new roots, make a cut at least two-thirds into the stem upwards at a sharp angle. Insert a piece of wood into the cut so that it cannot grow together again, and then put wet moss, best of all sphagnum, into and around the cut, tie with a soft wire and keep the moss packing constantly moist or cover it with a sheet of plastic. When roots appear, which takes four to five weeks, cut off the top together with the moss packing and pot it up in a mixture of equal parts of leafmould, loam, peat and sand, or John Innes potting compost. In summer put the plant by an open window, water fairly frequently and feed regularly. In winter keep the plant in a light situation at a temperature of 10 to 12° C. (50 to 54° F.) though higher temperatures are also tolerated. In summer ficus will benefit by being moved out of doors to a sunny position and watered liberally at regular intervals.

Ficus elastica ROXB. CV. 'Variegata'

Fittonia COËM.

Acanthaceae

These are low perennial herbaceous plants with felted stems. The simple leaves have conspicuous coloured veins. The inflorescence is a terminal spike of single flowers borne in the axils of bracts. All the known species and varieties originate from Peru.

Best suited for cultivation as a house plant is the variety *Fittonia verschaffeltii* 'Argyroneura', which has a low creeping habit and rich green leaves, 1 to 2½ in. (3 to 6 cm.) long, with a dense network of silvery-white veins. The species *F. verschaffeltii* is a low herbaceous plant with lovely dark green leaves with red veins. It, too, has yellow flowers.

Fittonias are propagated by means of cuttings taken at any time of the year. Cuttings root rapidly under glass in a mixture of peat and sand at a temperature of 20° C. (68° F.). When rooted the cuttings are transferred to small shallow pots (several to a pot) in a mixture of four parts leafmould, two parts peat and one part sand, or a peat-based compost or John Innes with extra peat. Fittonias should be kept constantly in a warm and shaded position and are very rewarding plants for window glasshouses, indoor glass cases and terrariums, in which they are easily grown. The only things they do not tolerate are an unduly dry atmosphere and a low temperature of lengthier duration. From April until August they should be given a weekly application of liquid feed. They are particularly good for beginners who do not have much experience in growing plants.

Fittonia verschaffeltii COËM.

Guzmania RUIZ & PAV.

Bromeliaceae

These are terrestrial or epiphytic bromeliads with thick rosettes of stiff leaves. The flowers are borne in heads, spikes or panicles, and have attractively coloured bracts. There are some 80 to 90 known species, all native to South America and the West Indies. Only the smaller ones, however, are suitable for cultivation as house plants.

Guzmania minor has pale green leaves spreading to 12 in. (30 cm.) in length. The flowers are white with red bracts. *Guzmania* × 'Magnifica' also has short yellow-green leaves and red flowers enclosed in red bracts. As many species do not produce seeds propagation is mostly by division. Guzmanias should be repotted in spring or summer, at which time stronger offshoots with roots may be separated from the parent plant and potted up into correspondingly large pots in a mixture recommended for epiphytic bromeliads (page 15). In accordance with the conditions in their native environment they require shade, a moist atmosphere and a temperature of 20 to 30° C. (68 to 86° F.) during the growth period. In winter the temperature must not drop below 15° C. (59° F.). Guzmanias do not require a winter rest period and, therefore, it is best to keep the temperature at the usual level even at this time. Water should be supplied regularly but in smaller quantity, care being taken that the root ball does not become sodden. Guzmanias are particularly well suited to window glasshouses and indoor glass cases where temperature and humidity can be controlled and kept constant.

Guzmania × 'Intermedia'

Gynura CASS.   *Compositae*

These are herbaceous plants or semi-shrubs with alternate, entire leaves that are either glabrous or hairy. The flowers are small and coloured yellow or purplish. The 80 or so species of this genus are native to the warm regions of Asia, Africa and Australia.

Most commonly grown as a house plant is *Gynura procumbens* (syn. *G. sarmentosa*). Young plants are of upright habit, older ones are prostrate. The stems are very thin, the leaves sharply notched and covered with bluish-violet hairs. Propagation is by cuttings which may be taken at any time of the year, though preferably in spring. The cuttings root very rapidly even in peat alone at a temperature of 20° C. (68° F.). When they have made roots pot them up into a mixture of two parts leafmould, one part peat, one part loam and one part sand (or John Innes or a peat-based compost) and put by a closed window. Once they are well established cut back the tops and later pot on into larger pots. During the summer the plants should be placed by a window in partial shade and watered liberally. In winter they require a temperature of 12 to 15° C. (54 to 59° F.) and less water.

The young plants are the most attractive and for this reason it is recommended to propagate them by cuttings every year in spring. Young plants are very good planted several together in a pot. The illustrated species is a plant of trailing habit and can be grown in hanging baskets.

Gynura procumbens MERR. (syn. *G. sarmentosa* DC.)

Hedera L.
Ivy

Araliaceae

Ivies are woody climbing plants with thin stems bearing a large number of short tendrils. The stalked leaves are three to five lobed. The seven known species are native to Europe and Asia.

Many forms have been developed from the European species *Hedera helix*, and there are now more than 150 named varieties. The forms with small and variegated leaves are particularly well suited for cultivation as house plants. Propagation is only by cuttings, which may be taken at any time of the year; spring and summer, however, are the best time for pot plants. The cuttings will root not only in a glass of water, which should be changed weekly, but also in pots in a mixture of peat and sand. Cuttings of rarer species should be covered with a glass jar or plastic bag. After they have rooted they should be potted up, several cuttings to one pot. A suitable potting mixture is four parts compost and one part sand, or John Innes potting compost can be used. The pots should then be placed in a shady spot by a closed window, in summer by an open window. Older plants may be repotted in spring but this is generally done in August.

Ivy is grown in cooler rooms, in corridors and by windows with a northern exposure. It may be trained to climb in various ways or grown in hanging baskets. In summer, water liberally and give the plants an occasional dose of liquid feed. In winter, water moderately and keep the temperature between 6 and 15° C. (43 to 59° F.). If you are looking for an ornamental plant requiring little in the way of care then any one of the varieties of ivy is a good choice.

Hedera helix L. cv. 'Goldheart'

132

Hibiscus L.   *Malvaceae*

Hibiscus are trees or shrubs with lovely blooms and the genus comprises some 200 species native to the tropics and subtropics. Generally grown as a house plant is *Hibiscus rosa-sinensis* from India and China, the flowers of which are as much as 4 to 6 in. (10 to 15 cm.) across and come in a variety of colours. Spring (from March on) is the time for repotting and also the time when older plants are cut back to encourage the formation of new shoots which will bear a profusion of flowers. The parts removed are trimmed to a length of 3 in. (8 cm.) and used as tip cuttings, the remainder of the stem being cut up into sections with two leaves each. These are then inserted in sand in pots and covered with glass jars or plastic bags. If you wish to propagate only a few new plants then it is best to do so by air-layering — making a cut into the stem at a strong angle and packing a wad of moist sphagnum around the cut. Cuttings root within three weeks, after which they should be potted up into 3-in. (8-cm.) pots in a mixture of four parts leafmould, two parts loam and one part sand (or John Innes or a peat-based compost) and placed in a warm spot by a window. Later they should be moved on to larger 5-in. (13-cm.) pots and placed in full sunshine. In summer water the plants liberally and feed them regularly. Plantlets grown from cuttings taken in spring bear flowers as early as July; the blooms are borne in succession. During the winter keep the plants by a window at a temperature of 12 to 15° C. (54 to 59° F.) and water lightly. Hibiscus bears lovely orchid-like blooms.

Hibiscus rosa-sinensis L.

Hippeastrum HERB.

Amaryllidaceae

These are bulbous perennials with strap-shaped leaves and large trumpet-shaped flowers. They include both evergreen species and ones whose leaves wither and die during the resting period. The 60 or so species of the genus are native to tropical America.

Propagation is by offsets of the bulb as well as by seed, which should be sown as soon as it is ripe. When flowering has finished in March or April repot the plants into a mixture of two parts leafmould, two parts loam and one part sand (or John Innes or a peat-based compost), the size of the pot depending on the size of the bulb — there should be a space of about ¾ in. (2 cm.) between the bulb and the edge of the pot. The bulb should be inserted so that the top half is above the surface. Small bulblets can be put in 3-in. (8-cm.) pots. After repotting the plants should be put by a closed window in a spot that is warm and light and water should be supplied moderately. In mid-June they may be put in an open window in full sunlight. Established plants should be given a light application of liquid feed once a week. From mid-August limit watering and from October withhold water altogether. When the leaves have yellowed and dried remove them from the plant and store the bulbs in a dark place at a temperature of 16 to 18° C. (60 to 65° F.). As soon as buds appear on the side of the bulbs move them back to a spot that is warm and light and resume watering. The plants will bloom within a short time.

Hippeastrum-Hybrid

Hoya R. BR.
Wax Flower

Asclepiadaceae

The genus *Hoya* embraces some 100 species native to tropical Asia and Australia. They include evergreen shrubs and prostrate plants as well as epiphytes and are distinguished by their thick ovate leaves. The star-shaped flowers are borne in umbels in the axils and look as if they have been moulded in wax.

Mainly grown as house plants are the species *Hoya carnosa* and *H. bella,* which have magnificent blooms and lovely foliage. Wax flowers are propagated by cuttings, preferably taken in spring. The cuttings, with one or two pairs of leaves, should be inserted in sand and the pot placed in a spot that is warm and light. Rooted cuttings of *H. carnosa* should be potted up into 3-in. (8-cm.) pots in a mixture of four parts leafmould, two parts loam and one part sand. *H. bella* cuttings should be put in a mixture for epiphytes — two parts peat and one each of pine leafmould, *Polypodium,* and pine-bark fibre — three cuttings to each shallow pan. Both species can also be potted in John Innes or a peat-based compost. *H. carnosa* should be potted on into larger pots in the summer. Place it in a sunny position in the window. Older specimens flower from May until November. Water liberally in summer and supply liquid feed every two weeks. In winter both species should be kept at a temperature of 10 to 12° C. (50 to 54° F.) and watering should be limited. Younger plants should be repotted every spring, older specimens every two or three years. Both *H. carnosa* and *H. bella* are rewarding species that are very good as house plants.

Hoya carnosa R. BR. 'Variegata'

138

Hydrangea L. *Hydrangeaceae*

The lovely shrubby hydrangeas are plants with opposite leaves and flowers (with coloured calyces) arranged in cymes or panicles. The 80 or so species of this genus originate from America and the warm regions of Asia.

The only one grown as a pot plant is *Hydrangea hortensis* from Japan and China. The flower heads are coloured red, pink or white. From the pink forms it is sometimes possible, under certain circumstances, to obtain blue kinds. Hydrangeas are propagated in spring by means of cuttings. When shoots growing from the root ball have reached a height of 2½ in. (6 cm.) cut them off, insert them in moist sand in pots and cover them with glass jars or plastic bags. At a temperature of 20° C. (68° F.) they will root within three weeks, after which they should be potted up into 3-in. (8-cm.) pots in a mixture of equal parts of rough peat and pine leafmould (or John Innes or a peat-based compost) and placed by a closed window. In mid-June they should be potted on into larger pots. During the summer months they can be placed by an open window or, better still, plunged into soil in the garden or put on the balcony. They should be watered liberally at this time and also given an occasional application of liquid feed. Before the first frost move them to a cool shed where they will shed their leaves. In March, place them once again in full sun by a window and water them as required so that there is always some water in the dish. After the flowers have faded repot the plants and move them out to the balcony or the garden. They may also be planted out of doors permanently.

Hydrangea hortensis SM.

Impatiens L.
Touch-me-not

Balsaminaceae

These are herbaceous plants with succulent stems, simple alternate leaves and flowers in a wide variety of colours. There are more than 550 known species native to tropical and subtropical Asia.

Most commonly cultivated as a house plant is the busy lizzie, *Impatiens walleriana*. This is a small shrub, growing to a height of 20 in. (50 cm.), with carmine-red flowers or with striped stalks and vermilion or pink flowers. Propagation is by means of cuttings, which root very easily and may be taken at any time of the year. Because of their rapid growth cuttings are generally taken from older specimens in the spring. They will root either in sand in a pot covered with a glass jar or simply in water. After making roots they should be potted up into 3-in. (8-cm.) pots and later potted on into 5-in. (13-cm.) pots in a mixture of loam and sand, or John Innes or a peat-based compost. In summer they prefer a position by a north-facing window and in winter by a window facing south. In winter they will survive in a room with a temperature of 10° to 12° C. (50 to 54° F.). From March to April they should be watered abundantly and given a weekly application of feed. Nearly all species have both tall and short forms. Their rapid rooting and ease of cultivation make them particularly good plants for beginners. Impatiens are profusely flowering plants which bear blossoms from early spring until autumn and sometimes even in winter.

Impatiens walleriana HOOK. (syn. *I. holstii* ENGL. & WARB., *I. sultani* HOOK b.)

142

Ixora L.

The more than 150 species of *Ixora* are flowering shrubs or trees native to the tropics. Best known is *Ixora coccinea* from the East Indies. The scarlet flower heads, which appear in summer, resemble those of the hydrangea but the blossoms are not as large.

Ixora may be propagated by means of cuttings which will root within four weeks in a warm propagator, but it is preferable to obtain and start out with larger, more robust plants. Ixoras require a warm, moist atmosphere and light position sheltered from the mid-day sun. In spring they should be cut back slightly and potted on into a mixture of four parts leafmould, two parts peat, two parts loam and one part sand, or a peat-based compost or John Innes with extra peat may be used. After repotting they should be provided with greater warmth, 20° C. (68° F.), watered with care and sprayed frequently. Once they are established, particularly during the flowering period, the plants should be given a light application of feed. When flowering is finished they require a six-week period of rest, at which time watering should be limited and feeding stopped, the plants sprayed frequently and kept at a temperature of 15° C. (59° F.). In winter and until the middle of April they require abundant sun, later, however, they should be sheltered from sun. In an excessively dry environment ixoras are often attacked by pests. Their cultivation is not easy and they are not, therefore, particularly good plants for the amateur.

Ixora coccinea L.

Jacobinia NEES EX MORIC.   *Acanthaceae*

Jacobinias are mostly herbaceous plants or shrubs with large entire leaves. The narrow tubular flowers, borne in the axils of ornamental bracts, form terminal spikes or panicles. The 30 or so species are natives of tropical America. Most common is *Jacobinia carnea*, which bears fairly long pinkish-red or flesh-pink flowers in July and August. Propagation of both this, and the illustrated *J. pohliana*, is by cuttings of young shoots, preferably taken in March. Place the shoots in a pot of sand and cover with a glass jar or plastic bag. They will root rapidly at a temperature of 20° C. (68° F.). Pot up rooted shoots in 3-in. (8-cm.) pots in a mixture of equal parts of loam, peat and sand (or John Innes potting compost) and place by a closed window until they are well rooted. In May pot them on into larger pots. In summer they may be kept in an open window as they tolerate brighter sun; water them liberally but do not feed as this would lead to too lush growth. Remove faded flowers. Jacobinias should be wintered indoors in a light position at a temperature of 14 to 16° C. (58 to 60° F.) and given water sparingly. Only one-year-old, or at most two-year-old plants are grown in rooms as these are more attractive. Jacobinias are lovely pot plants of easy culture which pose no problems even for the beginner.

Jacobinia pohliana LINDAU

Kalanchoë ADANS.   *Crassulaceae*

These are succulent herbaceous plants or semi-shrubs with fleshy, opposite, entire, leaves which may be stalked or sessile, and clusters of white, yellow or red blooms. The 150 or so species originate from tropical Asia and Africa. Most commonly grown is *Kalanchoë blossfeldiana* from Madagascar.

Amateur growers propagate kalanchoës by means of cuttings but nurserymen increase them by seed. In spring, when flowering has finished, remove the faded parts and after about a month's rest repot the plant, which will soon put out new shoots. When these are 2 to 2½ in. (5 to 6 cm.) long cut them off and put them in a dish with sand. Give them a good watering and place the dish by a closed window. To obtain bushier plants pot up rooted cuttings in threes into 3-in. (8-cm.) pots in a mixture of equal parts of leafmould, loam and sand (or John Innes potting compost with extra sand) and place the pots by a window. When they have grown and become stronger pot them on into 4-in. (10-cm.) pots. In summer they should be kept in a sunny spot by an open window and watered liberally. In August give them an occasional application of liquid feed. The plants should be overwintered in a light spot at a temperature of 15° C. (59° F.). At this time limit watering but take care that soil does not become too dry. As the days grow longer increase the amount of water. The flowering period is from January to April.

Kalanchoë blossfeldiana v. POELLN.

Lycaste LINDL.

There are approximately 35 species of *Lycaste,* mostly epiphytic orchids, though some are terrestrial, native to tropical and sub-tropical America. From the short, egg-shaped bulb grow one or two large thin leaves, which are shed every year, and from the base arise solitary blooms on short skalks. All species have fragrant flowers. These orchids are very good for house plant cultivation but are not suitable for cutting because of the short stalks. After flowering they should be repotted into a mixture suitable for terrestrial orchids (page 14) and then kept at a temperature of 16 to 18° C. (60 to 65° F.). Even older bulbs readily produce buds from which new bulbs and leaves grow. To obtain new plants these new bulbs may be separated from the old when repotting. More robust and stronger plants may be propagated by division of clumps. During the growing period, when they are putting out numerous new roots, the plants should be watered regularly and given a weekly application of a weak solution of organic feed. Place them by a window in partial shade. When growth has ceased and the bulbs have ripened, which is usually in the autumn, withhold water and move the plants to a cooler location with a temperature of 10 to 12° C. (50 to 54° F.). Resume watering in spring when the buds start to develop.

Lycaste aromatica LINDL.

Monstera SCHOTT.

Swiss Cheese Plant

These are handsome climbing plants with aerial roots. The leaves, borne on long stalks in two rows, are heart shaped and serrated and often also perforated with holes; young leaves have entire margins. There are some 30 species, all native to tropical America.

The most commonly grown is *Monstera deliciosa* from Mexico. It forms a strong, semi-woody stem with aerial roots reaching to the ground. The leaf stalks measure 12 to 20 in. (30 to 50 cm.) in length, the leaf blades are 16 to 32 in. (40 to 80 cm.) long and 12 to 24 in. (30 to 60 cm.) across and are coloured dark green. Monsteras cultivated indoors may grow to great heights. Older plants that have grown too large may be used for propagation. In spring cut off the tip together with three leaves and put in a pot, carefully twisting the aerial roots inside as well. Make cuttings of the remaining stem. Monsteras should be potted on in spring, before they begin making new leaves, into a mixture consisting of four parts leafmould, two parts loam, one part sand and bits of charcoal, or John Innes potting compost can be used. They are very tolerant of a dry atmosphere as well as dust. If placed near a window they develop strong leaves spaced close together but they are intolerant of direct sunlight. In summer they require abundant watering and regular feeding. In winter they should be kept at a temperature of 14 to 20° C. (58 to 68° F.) and watered lightly. The leaves should be washed regularly as dust collects on the large surface and clogs the pores.

Monstera deliciosa LIEBM.

Neoregelia L. B. SM.   *Bromeliaceae*

Neoregelias form spreading rosettes of leaves, the outer ones long and pointed, the ones in the centre short and splashed with colour. They are epiphytic and very hardy plants. Of the 34 or so known species, native to Brazil, it is the loveliest of them — *Neoregelia carolinae* 'Tricolor' — that is grown as a house plant. It is easily propagated by offsets which, once they have reached a convenient size, are separated from the parent plant when the latter is repotted in spring or summer. Put the offshoots into smaller pots in a mixture recommended for epiphytic bromeliads (page 15) and place the pots in the sun by a closed window. If put in a shaded position the plants will not develop their characteristic appearance; plants grown in stronger light have shorter leaves and are hardier.

Neoregelias are particularly good plants for rooms with low atmospheric moisture, as is found with central heating. They are especially beautiful during the flowering season when the leaves in the centre become coloured. If several species are cultivated then the grower will have flowering plants practically throughout the whole year. Light is a must, however, even in winter, at which time the plants should be kept at a temperature of 16 to 18° C. (60 to 65° F.) and watered moderately. Neoregelias are some of the most beautiful of house plants and not at all demanding in their requirements.

Neoregelia carolinae 'Tricolor' L. B. SM.

Nepenthes L.
Pitcher Plant

These are semi-shrubs with long stems and leathery, elliptic-lanceolate leaves the ends of which terminate in long tendrils bearing brightly coloured fly-catching pitchers topped by lids. The 75 species of *Nepenthes* are native to the tropics, originating mostly from Indonesia and Borneo. They are well-known insectivorous plants that catch not only insects but also small animals. A secretion containing pepsin is produced inside the pitcher, the drowned bodies of the insects decompose in this fluid and the plant absorbs the dissolved nutritive substances. Plants for cultivation in the home are usually bought at the florist's as propagation of nepenthes is very difficult. They should be grown in a window glasshouse or indoor plant case together with other tropical plants and in order to obtain well-developed pitchers the plants should be in a suspended position. During the growing period spray them in the daytime and occasionally give a weak solution of liquid organic feed. Hard water should never be used. Repot them every year in spring in a fresh mixture recommended for epiphytic orchids (page 14). In summer the plants require a temperature of up to 30° C. (86° F.) and in winter a temperature of at least 20° C. (68° F.). Repot the plants carefully as the roots are very delicate.

Nepenthes-Hybrid

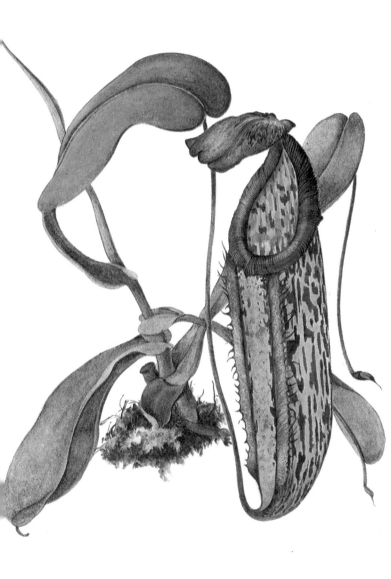

Odontoglossum KUNTH.   *Orchidaceae*

The 100 or so species of these epiphytic orchids grow wild at higher altitudes in tropical America — from Bolivia to Mexico. They have egg-shaped or pear-shaped, laterally flattened bulbs with one or more leaves. The long flower spikes grow upright but may sometimes be arching.

Odontoglossums should be repotted in early spring when they begin to develop new roots. Do not feed. The plants can be propagated by division when repotting. Use the smallest possible pots and fill them to at least half their depth with crushed crocks. Plants should be kept fairly dry for two or three weeks after repotting — until new roots begin to grow. From the end of May they will benefit from fresh air, so put them by a north-facing window, on a shaded porch or out of doors under a tree. Colder, damp air is harmful. The bulbs of some species are developed by the end of July and watering should be limited at this time. In the autumn put the plants in a light spot with a temperature of 15° C. (59° F.). As soon as flower buds appear on the underside of the bulbs begin watering again. Most species flower in November, December and January. It takes at least six weeks for the flower stem to reach its full growth and bear blooms. These should be removed before they have completely faded as flowering weakens the plant. Odontoglossums often do better in rooms than in the greenhouse.

Odontoglossum grande LINDL.

Pachystachys NEES

Acanthaceae

Pachystachys is a small evergreen shrub with simple opposite leaves and heads of flowers concealed in coloured bracts and carried at the ends of the branches. The genus contains about 7 species native to tropical South America. The stems are slender with drooping tips, the leaves are oblong and pointed.

In early spring cut back the parent plant moderately so that it will produce shoots. When these are about $2\frac{1}{2}$ in. (6 cm.) long separate them from the parent plant with a knife and prepare cuttings, which should be inserted in a pot in sand and covered with a glass jar or plastic bag. They will root very rapidly at a temperature of 18 to 20° C. (65 to 68° F.). Rooted cuttings should be potted up in threes into 3-in. (8-cm.) pots in a mixture of four parts leafmould, two parts loam and one part sand (or John Innes or a peat-based compost) and placed by a closed window. When they are firmly established they should be potted on into 5-in. (13-cm.) pots. During the summer they should be put in direct sunlight, watered liberally, and given a regular application of feed. In winter the plant should be kept in a well-lit place at a temperature of 12 to 15° C. (54 to 59° F.) and watered less frequently. If cut back in spring it will sprout nicely and flower profusely until summer.

Pachystachys lutea NEES

160

Pandanus L.
Screw Pine

These are lovely ornamental plants, either branching trees or shrubs, with slender palm-like stems and numerous aerial prop roots. The sword-like leaves are sheathed at the base and arranged in three or four rows. More than 200 species of these plants grow on the sea-coasts of tropical Asia, Africa and Australia. Numerous young shoots develop on the stem below the crown of leaves and these should not be separated from the parent plant while they are still young and soft. Wait until they are stronger, in some cases they may even have begun to make roots, then remove them and pot them up into small pots in a mixture of peat, sphagnum and sand. If this is done in spring the newly potted plants must be put in a warm spot, preferably in a window glasshouse; in summer they may be left standing freely in the room. When they have become established pot them on into 4-in. (10-cm.) pots in a standard mixture of equal parts of leafmould, loam and sand, or in John Innes potting compost. Then pot them on every spring, each time into a larger pot. Rooted plants should be given an occasional application of weak liquid feed. In winter limit watering and keep the temperature above 15° C. (59° F.). A light position is best for older plants, which will even tolerate sunlight. Screw pines are not suitable for small flats because they grow rapidly and take up too much space within a short time.

Pandanus veitchii hort. ex DALLIERE

Paphiopedilum PFITZ.
Lady Slipper

Lady slippers are terrestrial evergreen orchids. The young leaves are grooved and coloured green with a blue tinge; sometimes they are marbled. The solitary flowers are borne on a long stem. There are about 50 species of these orchids, all native to tropical and subtropical Asia, which are divided into three groups according to their temperature requirements: 1. those requiring a winter temperature of 7 to 10° C. (45 to 50° F.) e. g. *Paphiopedilum insigne* and its varieties; 2. those requiring a winter temperature of 12 to 16° C. (54 to 60° F.) e. g. *P. venustum, P.* × *leanum* (hybrid between *P. insigne* and *P. spicerianum*); and 3. those requiring a winter temperature of 20 to 22° C. (68 to 72° F.) e. g. *P. callosum* and *P. lawrenceanum.* Knowledge of temperature requirements and partial periods of vegetative rest of the various species is a must; if these conditions are not observed then the plants will flower only occasionally or not at all. Lady slippers may be propagated by division of clumps, but weak plants should not be divided. Spring is the best time for repotting. Warmth-loving species should be put in a mixture recommended for epiphytic orchids; one part lumpy clay can be added to this mixture for terrestrial species. Water sparingly and carefully after repotting, or, better still, only spray the plants. Place them in partial shade; put cold-loving species by the window and warmth-loving species in a window glasshouse or plant case. The watering of cold-loving species should be limited at the end of August but warmth-loving species should be kept in a warm and humid atmosphere throughout the year.

Paphiopedilum x *maudiae* HORT.

Passiflora L.
Passion Flower

Passion flowers are herbaceous plants, usually climbing vines that attach themselves to trees with their tendrils. The leaves are alternate, simple and palmate. The large showy flowers arise from a five-pointed calyx, which may be green or otherwise coloured, and have five stamens and three styles borne on a column-like projection. The genus *Passiflora* comprises more than 400 species native primarily to the warm regions of America, Asia and Australia. Loveliest of them all is *Passiflora coerulea* from Brazil.

Passion flowers should be repotted in spring and the plants cut back so that they will form new flower-bearing shoots. To make cuttings, cut the removed shoots into sections with two leaves each, put them in pots of sand and cover with glass jars or plastic bags. At a temperature of 20° C. (68° F.) they will root within three weeks, after which they should be potted up into 3-in. (8-cm.) pots in a mixture of equal parts of leafmould, peat, loam and sand (John Innes or a peat-based compost may also be used). Keep the pots warm by placing them by a closed south-facing window. When the plants are well rooted put them in full sunlight by a window. In June pot them on into larger pots and stake them. In summer they may be placed by an open window or on the balcony in full sun and should be watered liberally and fed. Passion flowers should be wintered at a temperature of 8 to 10° C. (46 to 50° F.) in a light spot and watered only slightly. They are hardly ever attacked by pests and diseases.

Passiflora coerulea L.

Pelargonium L'HÉRIT. ex AIT.   *Geraniaceae*

There are about 250 known species of *Pelargonium* originating mostly from South Africa, Asia and Australia. Most commonly grown as a house plant is *Pelargonium grandiflorum,* a semi-shrub, 8 to 36 in. (20 to 90 cm.) high, with a branching habit and a profusion of flowers each measuring up to $2\frac{1}{4}$ in. (6 cm.) in diameter.

Cultivation of large-flowered pelargoniums is different from that of other kinds. They are propagated in August after the flowers have faded. The tip cuttings, $2\frac{1}{4}$ to 3 in. (6 to 8 cm.) long and with ripe wood at the base, should not be allowed to wilt and should be put into small pots in a mixture of two parts peat, two parts loam and one part sand. Until they are well rooted keep them covered with a tall glass jar, then place them in a light position by a window in a room with a winter temperature of 10 to 12° C. (50 to 54° F.). Water moderately in winter. In March pot them on into 5-in. (13-cm.) pots in the mixture just described or in John Innes or a peat-based compost, and place them by a closed window. At the beginning of May put them in full sun, ventilate often and during the flowering period, from May until August, supply water liberally. Pelargoniums are often attacked by aphids and, therefore, the entire plant should be immersed before flowering in a solution containing a suitable insecticide. Because older plants grow very large it is recommended to propagate new plants from cuttings every year. Flowering plants of this species are just as beautiful as azaleas.

Pelargonium × *domesticum* L. H. BAILEY

Peperomia RUIZ et PAV. *Piperaceae*
Pepper Elder

Peperomias are evergreen perennials, some of which have trailing stems. The fleshy leaves, borne alternately or in whorls, have entire margins and often ornamental markings. There are about 600 known species, native to South America. These are some of the most widely cultivated low-growing house plants, and are very good planted several together in a bowl. They require little humidity and, therefore, do well even in homes with central heating. Peperomias are generally propagated by cuttings. Some species, e. g. *Peperomia obtusifolia, P. incana* and *P. serpens,* are increased by stem cuttings, and others, e. g. *P. argyreia* and *P. griseo-argentea,* by leaf cuttings. Stem cuttings should be trimmed to a length of $2\frac{1}{4}$ to 3 in. (6 to 8 cm.), leaf cuttings should be taken with a $1\frac{1}{2}$- to 2-in. (4- to 5-cm.)-long stalk. Both types of cuttings should be inserted in sand and they will root more rapidly if placed in a warm and light position. When they have rooted pot up stem cuttings into 4-in. (10-cm.) pots, two to three to a pot, and leaf cuttings singly into 3-in. (8-cm.) pots, moving these on later to 4-in. (10-cm.) pots. The mixture consists of two parts leafmould, two parts peat and one part sand, or John Innes seed compost with added leafmould may be used. Place the plants by a closed window and water sparingly, supplying feed once or twice a month. Give them more water after they are established. In winter peperomias require a light position by a window, a temperature of 18° C. (65° F.) and moderate watering. They are repotted in spring.

Pachystachys lutea E. MORR.

170

Phalaenopsis BL.
Butterfly Plant

Orchidaceae

The 40 or so species of these plants are widespread in Indonesia, the Philippines and New Guinea. They are bulbless epiphytic orchids with shortened stems, blunt, longish-ovate leaves and upright clusters of large blooms which are borne in succession and last a long time. Many hybrids have been developed which are very demanding in their requirements with regard to temperature and atmospheric moisture, particularly during the growing period. They do best in an artificially heated window glasshouse or plant case where the necessary temperature can be maintained even in more severe weather. The plants are grown in flat pans or the stronger ones in wooden baskets. They should be repotted in spring into a mixture recommended for epiphytic orchids but with a greater proportion of sphagnum; when repotting take care not to damage the roots. These orchids grow best when suspended and during the growing period they require a temperature of up to 30° C. (86° F.), frequent spraying and adequate shade. In cool summers heat should be supplied to the plants as they are sensitive to fluctuations in temperature. Rooted plants may be given a weak solution of liquid organic feed a few times during the summer. In winter, through to March, there is a period of partial rest during which time watering should be limited and the temperature lowered to 20° C. (68° F.).

Phalaenopsis amabilis BL.

Philodendron SCHOTT.

Araceae

There are about 200 species of *Philodendron,* all native to tropical America. They are climbing plants that produce aerial roots and have leaves which are often of unusual shapes and sizes. In tropical forests they grow in the shade of tree crowns.

Philodendrons may be propagated throughout the year but the best time for plants grown in rooms is spring or summer. Tip cuttings should be taken with two or three developed leaves and inserted singly in small pots in a mixture of leafmould, loam and sand in equal parts. The cuttings from climbers which have roots below each leaf are the quickest to root. Put the pots with the cuttings in a propagator or window glasshouse with a temperature of 22 to 25° C. (72 to 77° F.). Small cuttings may be covered with a glass jar. Older plants should be repotted in spring into a mixture of leafmould, loam and sand in equal parts.

In their native habitat philodendrons are fond of shade and even indoors may be put in a spot without direct sunlight. In summer the plants should be watered well and given a weekly application of feed. In winter, at lower temperatures, they should be watered slightly, only enough to keep the root ball from drying out. The winter temperature must not fall below 15° C. (59° F.). Philodendrons are repotted in spring or late summer every two or three years. They are handsome plants with many uses and are, therefore, very popular. Climbing and trailing forms may also be grown in hanging baskets and are exceptionally good for window glasshouses.

Philodendron imperiale SCHOTT
(syn. *P. asperatum* K. KOCH.)
young plant

Pilea LINDL.   *Urticaceae*
Friendship Plant, Aluminium Plant

The 200 species of this genus, native to the tropics, range in height
from tall to low growing or even prostrate plants. The opposite,
entire and slightly toothed leaves are the plants' chief attraction.

Most commonly grown as a house plant is *Pilea cadierei* from the
Congo with oval-oblong leaves with silvery-grey markings. It is
readily propagated by cuttings which root best in sand or water
at a temperature of 20° C. (68° F.). Cover cuttings with a glass jar
or place in a propagator. When they have put out roots pot them
up in twos in small pots in a mixture of two parts peat, two parts
leafmould and one part sand (or John Innes or peat-based compost)
and place them in semi-shade by a closed window. In summer pot
them on into 4-in. (10-cm.) pots. They grow fairly rapidly and during
the summer months should be kept in semi-shade by a window,
watered liberally and given an occasional feed. The winter temperature should be 14 to 18° C. (58 to 65° F.). In spring cut off the tips
for cuttings and discard the old plants — new young plants grow
rapidly and are more attractive. Young plants are good planted
several together in a bowl. Pilea, with its silvery markings, is also very
lovely arranged with green foliage plants. It is a good subject as it
is not difficult to grow or propagate.

Pilea cadierei GAGNEP. et GUILL.

176

Pinguicula L.
Butterwort

These perennial insectivorous plants with numerous roots and rosettes of fleshy, greasy leaves with entire margins are both unusual and interesting. The leaves curl up at the edges when touched and the greasy appearance is caused by countless narrow glands that produce a sticky secretion. The 40 species of this genus grow in damp locations and marshes, chiefly in the mountains of the northern hemisphere as well as in the Andes.

Two Mexican species, *Pinguicula caudata* and *P. gypsicola,* may be grown as house plants, but only in an environment with a moderate temperature. The plants grow best when plunged in a container of moist sphagnum in a terrarium or plant case. Pinguiculas should be repotted in spring at the start of the growing season into a mixture of two parts rough peat and one part old crumbled plaster or powdered brick. Older, stronger plants can be divided at this time. After repotting put them back in the terrarium. In summer the terrarium can be placed by the window and plenty of light is also necessary in winter when pinguiculas flower. In spring, before growth begins, break off some of the old leaves and insert them at an angle in the sphagnum. When they have made roots and a new young plant is formed at the base of each leaf, transfer them to pots.

Pinguicula caudata SCHLECHTEND.

Piper L.

Pepper

Peppers are climbing, evergreen shrubs with alternate entire leaves. The flowers are not pretty but the foliage is very attractive. About 600 species are distributed throughout the tropics but the two that are grown as house plants are *Piper nigrum* and *P. ornatum*.

Peppers are repotted in March and are propagated in the same way as climbing philodendrons and scindapsus — shoots may be cut up into sections so that each separated leaf has a piece of stem with a bud. The cuttings should be inserted in a mixture of peat and sand in a pot, covered with a glass jar or plastic bag and put in a warm place. When they have made roots pot them up in threes into 4-in. (10-cm.) pots in a mixture of two parts leafmould, two parts loam, one part peat and one part sand, or John Innes or a peat-based compost may be used.

Peppers may be grown in window glasshouses, in indoor glass cases or in large terrariums; *P. nigrum* may also be grown in hanging baskets as well as freely in the room. Inasmuch as they are plants of continually damp tropical forests all species require warmth, moisture and shade and must be supplied with these throughout the year. From March to August they should be fed every two weeks. If it is impossible to give them a winter temperature of about 16 to 18° C. (60 to 65° F.) then the root ball should be kept drier. Of the many species the easiest to grow is the lovely *P. nigrum*.

Piper ornatum N. E. BR.

Platycerium DESV.
Stag's Horn Fern

Polypodiaceae

There are about 18 species of these ferns which grow wild in the shady forests of Africa, Madagascar, southern India and Australia on the trunks of trees. They are epiphytic, heterophyllous ferns, i. e. they have two kinds of fronds, one infertile and usually rounded, the other green, forked like a pair of horns and carrying the spores.

These ferns are not repotted every year, all that is required is to topdress with some of the planting mixture at the beginning of the growth period. In older plants new plantlets grow from the adventitious buds on the roots and when these have formed two to three leaves cut them out, together with the root ball, and insert them in a mixture of two parts dry beech leaves, one part bits of peat previously soaked in a feeding solution, and one part polypodium roots, or in a mixture of equal parts of sphagnum and peat. They may be grown in flat pans as well as on a piece of hard wood. In summer water thoroughly, occasionally also giving a light application of liquid feed. During the growing season the ferns are fond of a warm moist atmosphere and slight shade. In winter a temperature of 15 to 18° C. (59 to 65° F.) will suffice. Indoors these ferns flourish if hung on walls near a window or on a glassed-in porch. Smaller specimens are also good for window glasshouses. Stag's horn fern is a lovely sight when planted in a hollow branch.

Platycerium hillii T. MOORE

Primula L.

Primulas are low-growing perennials with leaves arranged in a ground rosette and flowers borne in clusters. The 600 or so species grow mainly in the temperate zone of the northern hemisphere.

Most commonly grown as a house plant is *Primula obconica* from China, which has hairy leaves with toothed margins and pink, violet, blue, white or deep red flowers. For growing indoors purchase plants that are just beginning to flower and place them by a window with a northern or western exposure as the plants do not tolerate direct sunlight. In summer they may be stood by an open window and will require frequent watering and a light application of liquid feed now and then. In winter a cooler environment with a temperature of 10 to 12° C. (50 to 54° F.) is recommended. Remove faded flowers promptly to prevent seed formation. *P. obconica* is best left in its pot and not transferred, but should be given an application of feed in spring. It will produce attractive clusters of flowers for about two years, after which time it is preferable to purchase new, young plants. The hairy foliage of this species may cause a rash when touched. Cultivation of *P. sinensis* is the same as for *P. obconica*. *P. malacoides* should be purchased in February and put in a cool room in partial shade. It flowers from February to April and then dies. Propagation is by seeds.

Primula obconica HANCE

Pteris L.

These fairly tall ferns have pinnate or pinnately compound fronds with rows of sori (the spore-producing capsules) along the margins. The 60 or so species grow in the warmer regions, mainly in the tropics.

Most commonly cultivated as a house plant is *Pteris cretica* with long leathery leaves on upright 6- to 8-in. (15- to 20-cm.)-long stems. This fern has many different forms. Propagation is by division in spring and separated clumps should be put in a mixture consisting of two parts leafmould, two parts loam, two parts peat and one part sand. A peat-based compost or John Innes with extra peat may also be used. The size of the pot depends on the size of the roots. The newly repotted plants should be placed by a closed window and then during the growth period they should be watered liberally and given a light application of liquid feed. Indoors they grow well in a light position, though not in direct sunlight, best of all is a spot by a window with a western or northern exposure. Forms with green foliage will tolerate a winter temperature as low as 8 to 10° C. (46 to 50° F.) but those with variegated foliage require a winter temperature of 14 to 17° C. (58 to 63° F.). Smaller amounts of water should be given during the winter months.

Pteris ferns are not difficult to grow and are attractive both as solitary specimens or arranged with other plants. Young specimens are often put several together in a single container and later potted up into individual pots.

Pteris cretica L. var. *albo-lineata* hort.

186

Rhododendron L.   *Ericaceae*

The genus *Rhododendron* embraces more than 1,000 species mostly native to Asia, as well as Europe and America. They include evergreen shrubs with alternate entire leaves and flowers borne singly or in clusters.

The only species grown as a house plant is *Rhododendron simsii* (syn. *Azalea indica*). This flourishes in a cool and light position, being intolerant of a dry and warm atmosphere. It should be watered with soft or rain water and the root ball must never be allowed to dry out. If it becomes too dry the potted plant should be immersed in a pail of water and left to soak for several hours. Plants are transplanted when they have finished flowering, and must always have a damp root ball for this. Small plants should be potted on every year, older ones at several-year intervals. A suitable potting mixture is one consisting of two parts leafmould, two parts peat and one part sand. A peat-based compost or John Innes with extra peat may be used. In summer the plants will benefit by being put out of doors, best of all on a balcony or in the garden under a tree with the pot plunged in the soil. Well-rooted plants should be given a light application of liquid feed now and then. At the end of September, before the first light frosts, move the plant indoors again and put it in a cool spot by a window. The winter temperature should be 8 to 10° C. (46 to 50° F.).

Rhododendron simsii PLANCH. (syn. *Azalea indica* L.)

Rhoeo HANCE EX WALP.   *Commelinaceae*
Boat Lily

This genus has only the single species *Rhoeo spathacea* (syn. *R. discolor*) from Mexico. This is a plant of upright habit with a short fleshy stem and pointed lanceolate leaves, glossy and olive green above and violet on the underside. The small white flowers are insignificant. There is a variegated form — *R. spathacea* 'Vittata' with golden-yellow-striped leaves.

Rhoeo is easily propagated by tip as well as lateral cuttings and also by means of seeds. The cuttings should be inserted in small pots in sandy leafmould; if taken in the spring they need to go into a warm propagator or window glasshouse, if taken in the summer they can be placed by a closed window. The cuttings root fairly rapidly and when they have done so they should be potted on into larger, 4- or 5-in. (10- to 13-cm.) pots. Rhoeo bears an abundance of flowers and forms seeds without artificial pollination. Seeds should be sown in pans of compost and young seedlings potted up into small pots and later moved to larger pots. The plant should be repotted every year in spring or summer into a mixture of loamy soil, leafmould and sand, or John Innes or a peat-based compost may be used. In winter it requires a light position by a window and temperature of 15° C. (59° F.), in summer partial shade and liberal watering is necessary as well as an occasional application of feed.

Rhoeo is a lovely ornamental plant which may be grown as a solitary specimen or placed in a group with other plants. The genus *Rhoeo* is a relation of and similar in appearance to the genus *Tradescantia*.

Rhoeo spathacea STEARN 'Vittata'

Rochea DC.

These are succulent plants with attractive flowers. The four species are natives of South Africa and the best known is *Rochea coccinea,* which has crimson flowers borne in thick clusters. Propagation is by cuttings, preferably taken in March or April. These should be about 2 in. (5 cm.) long and if inserted in a mixture of peat and sand and placed in a light spot at a temperature of 15 to 18° C. (59 to 65° F.) they will root rapidly. They can then be potted up into 3-in. (8-cm.) pots, singly or in groups of three, in a mixture consisting of two parts of loam, one part of leafmould and one part of sand (or John Innes potting compost with extra sand) and placed by a window. At the beginning of June put them in direct sun by an open window. In late June pinch the tips to encourage branching and pot the plants on into larger pots. When they have become established water more liberally and in the autumn give them an application of a phosphate fertilizer to help the formation of flowers. In winter put the plants by a window; the temperature at this time may be as low as 3° C. (37° F.) and water should be applied sparingly. As the days lengthen in spring the supply of water can be increased. The flowering period is in April and May and after flowering has finished the parent plant should be cut back and repotted. It needs to be placed by a window at first, but later, from June until the autumn, it will benefit by being moved out of doors.

Rochea coccinea DC.

Saintpaulia H. WENDL.
African Violet

Gesneriaceae

African violets are low-growing herbaceous perennials, often with practically no stems, forming rosettes of fleshy, ovate, long-stalked leaves and bearing dainty flowers arranged in sparse clusters (dichasiums). There are about 11 species native to tropical East Africa but the best known is *Saintpaulia ionantha*. This species has violet-blue flowers but many varieties are available, both single and double, in shades of pink and white.

Saintpaulia ionantha is increased by means of leaf cuttings at any time of the year. The leaves should be taken with 2½- to 3-in. (6- to 8-cm.)-long stalks from healthy, richly flowering plants and inserted vertically in pans in a mixture of equal parts of peat and sand and then watered thoroughly. They will root within six weeks at a temperature of 20 to·22° C. (68 to 72° F.) and a young plantlet will develop at the base of each leaf stalk. When the cuttings take root pot them into 2½-in. (6-cm.) pots in a mixture of two parts leafmould, two parts peat and one part sand (or a peat-based compost or John Innes with extra peat) and place them in a warm room in partial shade. During their growth, they should be repotted twice; first into 3-in. (8-cm.) pots and later into 4-in. (10-cm.) ones.

During the summer the best position for the plants is by a north-facing window because too much light causes yellowing of the leaves. As a rule, African violets grow and bear flowers throughout the year and thus require moderate watering and a temperature of 18 to 20° C. (65 to 68° F.) even in winter. Give them a feed once or twice a month during the flowering period.

Saintpaulia ionantha H. WENDL.

Sansevieria THUNB.
Mother-in-Law's Tongue

Sansevierias are plants with short, thick underground stems and stiff, fleshy, lance-shaped leaves, often decoratively mottled. There are some 60 species native to tropical Africa and India. Species with green foliage are propagated by leaf cuttings, those with variegated foliage by division. Cut old mature leaves crosswise into $2\frac{1}{2}$-in. (6-cm.)-long sections and insert these in pans in a mixture of one part peat and two parts sand. At a temperature of 20 to 22° C. (68 to 72° F.) they will root and produce new shoots within two months, and they can then be transferred into 3-in. (8-cm.) pots (three or four cuttings to a pot) in a mixture of two parts leafmould, one part loam and one part sand. John Innes potting compost may also be used. Variegated species are increased by division of the clumps. This is done before repotting in spring when well developed leaves, together with a section of the underground stem, are removed and placed in shallow pots with good drainage. The plants are kept in a warm spot and watered sparingly.

Sansevierias are lovely ornamental plants that do not take up much room. They need a light position throughout the year and will tolerate a dry atmosphere, and are, therefore, very good for homes with central heating. In winter water should be supplied according to the ambient temperature; if it drops below 15° C. (59° F.) then water is withheld altogether. Never use cold water directly from the tap. Variegated species are more demanding with regard to temperature and watering. Older plants are repotted at two-year intervals, young plants every year in spring.

Sansevieria trifasciata PRAIN 'Hahnii'

Saxifraga L.   *Saxifragaceae*

Saxifrages are mostly herbaceous perennials with variously shaped leaves often forming a ground rosette. There are about 300 species growing throughout the world but the one cultivated as a house plant is the ornamental *Saxifraga stolonifera* from China. The leaves are orbicular and long stalked, whitish above and with reddish veining on the underside. Red shoots grow between the leaves and these bear small plantlets used for propagation. A very lovely form is *S. stolonifera* 'Tricolor', with leaves coloured white, reddish and green, which should be repotted at the end of winter. It can be increased at any time of the year by removing the plantlets that grow between the leaves and inserting them in sandy soil in small pots which are then placed by a closed window. Later they can be potted on into 4-in. (10-cm.) pots. In summer this species should be kept in semi-shade by an open window, on the balcony or in the garden. It requires more water at this time and a weekly application of feed. In winter it benefits by being kept in a cool room at a temperature of 6 to 10° C. (43 to 50° F.) and water should be supplied sparingly. Saxifrages are most attractive if positioned so that the ornamental stolons hang freely downwards. The variegated form requires a winter temperature of 15° C. (59° F.).

Saxifraga stolonifera MEERB. (syn. *S. sarmentosa* L. f.)

Scindapsus SCHOTT.
Ivy Arum

These climbing plants with their heart-shaped leaves, either a rich shining green or streaked with cream or yellow, make lovely ornamental house plants. The 20 or so species are natives of tropical Asia.

Generally grown indoors is *Scindapsus aureus* with smooth green leaves streaked with yellow. Scindapsus should be repotted every two or three years and can be increased at any time of the year, though preferably in spring, by means of cuttings. Tip cuttings should be taken with two or three developed leaves, stem cuttings with just one leaf. Insert the cuttings in a pan in a mixture of peat and sand and cover with a glass jar or plastic bag. If the rooting medium is kept at a temperature of 20 to 22° C. (68 to 72° F.) the cuttings will root within a short time and can then be moved on to 4-in. (10-cm.) pots (three to five to a pot) containing a mixture of four parts rich leafmould and one part sand (or John Innes or a peat-based compost) and put in a warm room by a closed window. If the plants are well rooted they will benefit from a light application of liquid feed. Scindapsus should be kept in a shady spot by a closed window even in summer. The optimum winter temperature is 20° C. (68° F.). Scindapsus may be grown in hanging baskets or tied and trained to grow upright against a wall. This is a hardy, long-lived plant which grows well indoors. Recently *S. aureus* was renamed *Rhaphidophora aurea*.

Scindapsus pictus HASSK.

Senecio L.
Cineraria

There are about 1300 species of cinerarias distributed throughout the world but the only one grown as a house plant is *Senecio cruentus* (syn. *Cineraria cruenta*) from the Canary Islands. English, German and French growers have developed many forms which are distinguished by their low growth and masses of lovely flowers in a wide variety of shades. They are propagated commercially from seed.

For home decoration plants should be purchased at the end of February before they begin to flower and placed in a cool room by a window. For good growth they require a cool, moist atmosphere and will soon die in a warm environment. Before flowering, examine the plants for pests, particularly aphids. During the flowering period water should be supplied liberally with liquid feed added every now and then. Cinerarias flower in early spring and if placed in a suitable spot and given the necessary care they will flower for a number of weeks. When flowering has finished the plants die so it is necessary to purchase new ones each year. Many garden forms are cultivated in a wide range of bright colours.

Senecio cruentus-Hybrid

Sinningia NEES.
Gloxinia

Gloxinias are herbaceous plants with tuberous underground stems. The leaves are opposite and the symmetrical trumpet-shaped flowers are borne singly. The 20 or so species are native to Brazil.

Most commonly grown as a house plant is *Sinningia*-Hybrid, the gloxinia. In nurseries it is propagated from seed or from tubers but propagation by means of tubers in the only feasible one in the home. At the beginning of March remove any old roots from the tubers which should then be planted close together, so that only their tips show, in a pan or seed tray in a mixture of two parts peat and one part sand. Place the pan in a warm room [20 to 22° C. (68 to 72° F.)] by a window. When the young shoots are about 2 in. (5 cm.) high remove the tubers together with the root ball and pot them up in suitably sized pots in a mixture of four parts peat, two parts leafmould and one part sand, or in John Innes or a peat-based compost. The potted plants should be placed in a warm, light spot by a window but shielded from direct sunlight. Water them with tepid water and when they have become established give them an occasional application of liquid feed. Rainwater or boiled water is best. If purchasing plants select only those that have lots of flower buds. When flowering has finished limit the watering and after the leaves have yellowed store the tubers in their pots in a moderately warm spot. Put them out again in spring and proceed as previously described.

Sinningia-Hybrid

Stapelia L.

Starfish Flower, Toad Flower

Asclepiadaceae

Stapelias are leafless, succulent plants with quadrangular stems, 4 to 12 in. (10 to 30 cm.) long and about ½ in. (1 cm.) thick. The fantastically lovely star-shaped flowers, which have an unpleasant smell, appear at the base of the stems in summer. There are about 120 species, all native to Africa.

Propagation is by vegetative means as well as by seed. When repotting plants in spring remove weaker shoots and put them in 3-in. (8-cm.) pots, several to a pot, in a mixture of four parts leafmould, two parts loam, one part charcoal and one part sand. Fill the pots to one-third of their depth with crushed crocks to provide good drainage. The following year move the shoots to flat, shallow pans so they have room to spread and prepare for flowering.

In summer put stapelias in a light position near a window but avoid direct sunlight. Water liberally and apply liquid feed every two weeks. In the autumn, when growth ceases, limit watering; however, if the roots are allowed to become too dry they wither and lose their ability to absorb water whereupon they decay when they are watered and the plant dies. In winter stapelias should be kept in a light spot by a window at a temperature of 10° C. (50° F.) and watered moderately. Because they tolerate a dry atmosphere they can be grown with comparative ease in homes with central heating and for this reason are quite popular. They should be repotted every year. Even when not in flower stapelias are attractive ornaments, as are other succulents grown as house plants.

Stapelia variegata L.

Streptocarpus LINDL.   *Gesneriaceae*
Cape Primrose

These are herbaceous plants with one or more leaves at ground level
from the axils of which grow the flowers, either singly or in clusters.
These may be large or small, coloured purple, blue, pink or white.
There are some 80 species of this genus native to South Africa.

The most commonly grown as a house plant is *Streptocarpus*-Hybrid,
which, with its profusion of blooms, is as lovely as the gloxinia and
a good plant for indoor cultivation. The Cape primrose is propagated
mostly by seeds which should be sown in February or March on
peat, covered with a glass jar or plastic bag and given a temperature
of 20° C. (68° F.). Once they have germinated the seedlings should
be pricked out into another pan containing a mixture of four parts
peat, two parts leafmould and one part sand (or John Innes or
a peat-based compost) and placed in a warm spot by a window.
When the seedlings become crowded pot them up individually into
$2\frac{1}{2}$-in. (6-cm.) pots containing the same mixture and later in summer
pot them on into larger, 4-in. (10-cm.) pots. They should be kept
by a closed window with a northern exposure. The plantlets begin
flowering in August and continue until November but the blossoms
are not as tender as those of gloxinias. In winter, a temperature
of 12 to 14° C. (54 to 58° F.) and a moderate supply of water will
be sufficient. Repot in spring. Older specimens bloom from April
throughout the summer.

Streptocarpus-Hybrid

Syngonium SCHOTT.
Goose Foot

There are some 14 species of this genus, native to the area extending from the West Indies to Mexico and Brazil. They are climbing plants with long stems and aerial roots and leaves which have long stalks and are three, five to nine fingered. The spathe is yellowish to whitish green.

One species commonly grown as a house plant is *Syngonium podophyllum,* native to tropical America. It needs a higher temperature and very moist atmosphere and for this reason the pot should be stood on pebbles or pieces of coke in a dish of water. If the plant forms aerial roots then this is an indication that it has sufficient moisture. Syngoniums may grow too tall, and in this case it is advisable to cut off the tips — up to 12 in. (30 cm.) in length — together with the aerial roots and insert the cuttings into pots in a mixture of four parts leafmould, two parts peat and one part sand. (A peat-based compost may also be used.) The base of the parent plant will put out new shoots. Syngonium can also be trained up a moss-filled cone of wire netting or grown in a soilless medium. It does not have a dormant period and should, therefore, be kept in a warm, moist atmosphere throughout the year and given a weekly application of feed.

The genus *Syngonium* includes lovely ornamental house plants very similar to philodendrons, for which they are often mistaken. Both syngoniums and philodendrons belong to the family *Araceae. S. podophyllum* is a good species for amateur growers.

Syngonium podophyllum 'Albolineatum'

Tillandsia L.   *Bromeliaceae*

Tillandsias are mostly epiphytic bromeliads of widely varied shape and habit with linear leaves arranged in a rosette. The trimerous flowers are carried in terminal spikes and show marked variation in size and colour, which may be blue, violet, yellow, and sometimes even reddish or greenish. The more than 400 species of *Tillandsia* are natives of South America. Being epiphytic plants they are adapted to harsher environmental conditions and are, therefore, very good for indoor cultivation. The flowering period is fairly long for the flowers are borne in succession.

Tillandsias are divided into two groups according to where they grow. The first are epiphytes that grow in humus in the forks of trees, e. g. *Tillandsia lindenii, T. tricolor, T. cyanea* and their cultivation is the same as for *Vriesea*. The second group includes epiphytes growing on the bark of trees and raising these from the seed is very difficult. It is better to get hold of a twig covered with the plants if at all possible. Epiphytic tillandsias of the second group are true gems of the window glasshouse or plant case. It is preferable to use rainwater for watering. The required temperature is the same as for other plants cultivated in window glasshouses.

Tillandsia cyanea MORR.

Vallota SALISB. EX HERB.   *Amaryllidaceae*
Scarborough Lily

The only existing species of the genus *Vallota* is *V. speciosa* from South Africa. This has a brown, egg-shaped bulb from which arise 12- to 16-in. (30- to 40-cm.) -long leaves measuring ¾ to 1 in. (2 to 2.5 cm.) across. The flower stalk, about 10 in. (25 cm.) tall, grows from the centre of the leaves and is terminated by trumpet-shaped flowers arranged in an umbel. More robust specimens often produce several such stalks. The flowers are a brilliant vermilion and measure up to 3 in. (8 cm.) across.

Vallotas should be repotted every three to five years. Propagation is by seeds and by offsets of the bulb (bulblets); plants grown from bulblets develop more rapidly. As soon as leaves and roots form on the bulblets they should be separated from the parent plant so that it is not unnecessarily weakened, this is generally done in April when the plants are being repotted. Put two bulbs each into 3-in. (8-cm.) pot in a mixture of two parts leafmould, two parts loam and one part sand (or John Innes compost) and place them in a light spot by a closed window. When they have rooted water more liberally. In summer both young and older plants may be kept by an open window but they must be kept well watered and should be given liquid feed occasionally; in August watering should be limited. The plants flower in September. Vallota does not have a complete period of vegetative rest during the winter and at this time should be kept in a light place at a temperature of 8 to 10° C. (46 to 50° F.) and watered lightly.

Vallota speciosa VOSS.

Vanda R. BR.

This is an interesting group of epiphytic orchids numbering more than 50 species native to the monsoon region from India to New Guinea. The stem is stout, upright and thickly covered with leathery leaves, generally arranged in two rows, in the axils of which grow clusters of medium to large blooms.

These orchids should be repotted after the flowers have faded, but not every year, into a mixture for epiphytic orchids (page 14). In the case of plants that have grown too tall cut off any tips with well-developed aerial roots and pot them separately. Put crocks in the bottom of the pot for drainage and gradually fill the spaces between the roots with small portions of the compost. After being repotted the plants require more warmth and humidity, take care, however, not to spray the leaves and shade the plants if they are kept by a window. The growing period is from March till August and then the autumn and winter temperatures may be allowed to fall to as low as 12 to 14° C. (54 to 58° F.). Some species, such as *Vanda coerulea*, begin flowering in December; these should be kept in a warmer spot and watered moderately. The others flower in March and April. Growth begins again after the flowers have faded. To keep the roots from growing out to the side tie them with raffia so that they grow downwards as this makes them easier to fit in the pot when repotting.

Vanda tricolor LINDL.

Vriesea LINDL. mut BEER

Vrieseas are mostly epiphytic plants with abbreviated stems bearing rosettes of broad, smooth, green leaves either marbled or marked with horizontal bands. The flower spikes are large and have beautifully coloured bracts. The more than 100 species originate from South and Central America.

Vrieseas do not have a dormant period and small species grow best in a window glasshouse or plant case. Plants are repotted in spring, after the removal of any offshoots, into a compost recommended for epiphytic bromeliads and, because the root system is negligible, they should be put in small pots. Vrieseas do not make many offshoots, generally only one or two after flowering has finished. Remove faded parts when the offshoots have reached a good size. In summer the plants need partial shade. Certain, more robust species are equally effective grown as solitary specimens or planted on epiphytic logs or branches. Green-leaved species may be overwintered at a temperature of 15° C. (59° F.) with limited watering. Variegated species, including *Vriesea splendens,* require a winter temperature of at least 18 to 20° C. (65 to 68° F.). Because they need a moist atmosphere they benefit by frequent spraying with tepid water. Vrieseas are the most commonly grown bromeliads because the horizontally banded leaves of some are just as ornamental as the beautiful flower spikes.

Vriesea splendens LEM.

Zebrina SCHNIZL.

Commelinaceae

Zebrinas are perennial plants with prostrate stems and oval stalkless leaves. The four species that belong to the genus are native to Mexico and the one most commonly grown is *Zebrina pendula,* which is readily increased by means of stem cuttings, the same as the related tradescantia. Take 3-in. (8-cm.)-long cuttings from the tips of older, unsightly plants and insert them in 5-in. (13-cm.) pots, eight to ten to a pot. The best potting mixture is a sandy, semi-heavy garden soil. Given too rich a soil and too much moisture the colour of the leaves fades. If kept in a light spot they will grow into attractive ornamental plants, in shade, however, they tend to be weak with long stems. They are very good as companions to other plants in large, unattractive containers as they spread rapidly and conceal the containers. All zebrinas tolerate a dry atmosphere and are, therefore, suitable for homes with central heating. In winter they should be kept in a light spot at a temperature of 12 to 15° C. (54 to 59° F.). In summer they may be planted out in boxes on the balcony or in the garden. In the autumn cut off the tips and use them for propagation. Zebrinas have pink flowers but their most attractive feature is their beautifully coloured foliage, the same as in the case of tradescantias.

Zebrina pendula SCHNIZL. 'Quadricolor'

Zygocactus K. SCHUM.   *Cactaceae*
Christmas Cactus

These plants are distinguished by their flat lobster-claw-like shoots and flowers which are borne at the ends of the stems. In their native habitat they grow on trees like epiphytes. Altogether there are about five species originating from Brazil.

Propagation is by cuttings or grafting. Cuttings comprising two of the leaf-like segments should be inserted in sand in a pot, where they will soon root at a temperature of 18 to 20° C. (65 to 68° F.). Pot up rooted cuttings in threes into 3-in. (8-cm.) pots in a mixture of four parts leafmould, two parts peat and one part sand and put them by a closed window. Water sparingly. In summer put older plants by an open window in partial shade, water more liberally and give them two or three applications of a proprietary liquid feed. At the beginning of September limit the watering so that the stem segments will ripen and produce flowers. A suitable winter temperature is 12 to 15° C. (54 to 59° F.). As soon as buds appear at the ends of the stems the water supply can be slightly increased. After flowering has finished repot the plants. Zygocactus is a lovely ornamental plant, its greatest attraction being that it flowers in winter when there are few other flowering plants. To obtain specimens with overhanging crowns graft zygocactus on pereskia rootstock which has been started into growth in March. At room temperature the scion will fuse with the stock within three weeks and by the end of summer will have made a nice crown.

Zygocactus truncatus K. SCHUM. (syn. *Schlumbergera truncata*)

PLANTS FOR A SITUATION WITH WINTER
TEMPERATURE OF 18 TO 20° C. (65 TO 68° F.)

Partial Shade	Sunny Situation
Aglaonema	Ananas
Anthurium	Billbergia
Aphelandra	Codiaeum
Asplenium	Cryptanthus
Caladium	Neoregelia
Cocos	Pandanus
Cordyline	Piper
Dieffenbachia	Sansevieria
Dracaena	
Fittonia	
Guzmania	
Philodendron	
Platycerium	
Saintpaulia	
Scindapsus	
Syngonium	
Vriesea	

PLANTS FOR A SITUATION WITH WINTER
TEMPERATURE OF 12 TO 16° C. (54 TO 60° F.)

Partial Shade	Sunny Situation
Asplenium	Ardisia
Begonia	Asparagus
Cattleya	Beloperone
Cissus	Euphorbia
Cyperus	Ficus
Pilea	Fortunella
Primula	Gynura
Pteris	Hibiscus

Partial Shade	Sunny Situation
Rhoeo	Hoya
Saxifraga	Ixora
Vanda	Jacobinia
Zebrina	Rochea
	Stapelia

PLANTS FOR A SITUATION WITH WINTER TEMPERATURE OF 8 TO 12°C (46 TO 54° F.)

Partial Shade	Sunny Situation
Acorus	Abutilon
Camellia	Acacia
Clivia	Bougainvillea
Coelogyne	Drosera
Cyclamen	Hippeastrum
Cymbidium	Hydrangea
Fatshedera lizei hort.	Kalanchoë
Rhododendron	Passiflora
Senecio	Pelargonium
	Pinguicula
	Rochea
	Zygocactus

PLANTS FOR SITUATIONS SOME DISTANCE FROM THE WINDOW BUT WITH AMPLE LIGHT IN THE DAYTIME — TEMPERATURE 12 TO 18° C. (54 TO 65° F.)

Aglaonema   Aspidistra   Billbergia nutans   Billbergia windii
Hedera — ornamental species   Philodendron scandens   Syngonium

Dry or dusty rooms, or ones with coal-gas heating, impede the plant's basic life processes, primarily transpiration and photosynthesis, and in the long run not even the most painstaking care in cleaning the leaves can prevent damage to the plant.

PLANTS FOR THE WINDOW GLASSHOUSE AND INDOOR GLASS CASE WITH WINTER TEMPERATURE 18 TO 22° C. (65 TO 72° F.)
(South–facing windows should be provided with blinds to shield the plants in summer)

Bertonerila   Caladium   Fittonia   Guzmania   Nepenthes
Nidularium   Phalaenopsis   Platycerium — small species
Scindapsus   Tillandsia — including epiphytic species   Vriesea

PREVENTIVE CARE OF HOUSE PLANTS

Plant	Pest	Treatment
Abutilon, Aphelandra, Asparagus, Fuchsia, Gynura, Hibiscus, Hydrangea, Pelargonium	Mites *(Aphidoidea)* suck plant sap	Proprietary insecticides. Dosage according to instructions on the label
Abutilon, Acacia, Citrus, Codiaeum, Platycerium	Scale insects *(Coccoidea)* suck plant sap	
Abutilon, Achimenes, Azalea, Fuchsia, Pelargonium	White fly *(Aleyrodoidea)* suck plant sap	
Anthurium, Myrtus, Aspidistra, Azalea, Cissus, Fatsia, Hedera	Mites of the genus *Tarsonemus* suck plant sap	
Anthurium, Azalea, Camellia, Codiaeum, Ficus, *Orchidaceae*	Septoria fungi leaf-spot	Organic fungicides. Dosage according to instructions on the label
Crassula, *Bromeliaceae*, Sansevieria	Fusarium fungi leaf-spot	
Begonia, Cineraria, Hydrangea, Pelargonium	Mildew *(Erysiphales)* whitish coating on leaves	

INDEX OF COMMON NAMES

INDEX OF LATIN NAMES